I0569936

# Portraits of the Blues

**Darrell Arnold, Ph.D.**

**With portraits by Irena Gapkovska**

SISYPHUS PUBLISHING
SURFSIDE, FLORIDA

# Portraits of the Blues

**Darrell Arnold, Ph.D.**

© 2024 Darrell P. Arnold
Sisyphus Publishing

ISBN:
979-8-9910134-0-6 (PB)
979-8-9910134-1-3 (D)
979-8-9910134-2-0 (H-Lib)
979-8-9910134-3-7 (H)

Library of Congress Control Number: 2024913734

All rights reserved. No part of this publication may be reproduced in any form, by any electronic or mechanical means (including photocopying, recording, or information storage and retrieval) without permission in writing from the publisher.

The illustrations are originals created by the artist Irena Gapkovska. All rights to the images (copyright and moral rights) are fully retained by the artist. The images may not be reproduced in any form without the permission in writing from the artist. The images are used here with permission. Contact: www.ngoartstudio.org

Lyrics of Bessie Smith's "Backwater Blues" are in the public domain, Columbia © 1927. Permission to use the lyrics of Skip James are courtesy Adelphi Records Inc. & Blind Basement Music Publ. ASCAP.

Sisyphus Publishing, Surfside, FL
www.sisyphuspublishing.com
www.darrellarnold.com

Cover Design: Imagine Media Concepts

This book accompanies the Arco Records album, "Portraits of the Blues" by Darrell Arnold. Available to purchase through www.arcorecords.org and www.darrellarnold.com

*"Without music, life would be a mistake"*
*(Friedrich Nietzsche)*

*This book is dedicated to musicians and artists who write, play music and create artwork they love—even when they often see little in return. They make life more worth living. And as the lives of the country blues artists demonstrate, sometimes the small ripple effects of their labors of love gain a power transcending all expectations.*

# Contents

# Prologue

My first direct encounter with blues came long after I had come to love its musical progeny—soul, rhythm 'n' blues, rock'n'roll. I was born in North Platte, Nebraska—a small town sometimes known by those who have stopped there on their travels along Interstate 80 in central Nebraska. It houses Buffalo Bill's Wild West Ranch, the place Bill Cody called home for about 20 years of his life and from which he launched his Wild West Show. My parents had grown up on farms in central Nebraska about 80 miles from there. My father was a fan of Hank Williams, Gene Autry, Johnny Cash. He liked old time country better than later country. He sang a bit around the house, whistled, and on a rare occasion I heard him yodel. My mother played some piano and sang. Her brothers had been old time musicians, playing barn dances in central Nebraska small towns—Sumner, Eddyville, and Miller—songs like "Red River Valley." One uncle was an excellent saxophone player, who once had a chance to join the Tommy Dorsey orchestra. But he had ten children and a Catholic sense of familial responsibility. So he played music as a hobby. The family on both sides were country folk, from long lines of country folk in Ireland, Scotland, and England. I inherited some of their tastes, growing up in a large family with nine siblings in a large small town. In Flatrock, as our hometown is affectionately called, through older siblings I first heard blues influenced music from Eric Clapton, J.J. Cale, and George Thorogood.

It was as a graduate student in St. Louis in the 1980s and early 1990s that I first heard country blues. There I began to regularly go to shows of Tom Hall, a local country blues musician who regularly played at bars in St. Louis' Riverfront neighborhoods. Together with a friend of mine who had grown up with the advantages of hearing radio stations like WNYC in New York, I ventured out weekly to hear Tom's shows. The experience planted a seed: I wanted to learn the music of Mississippi John Hurt, Robert Johnson, Tommy Johnson—the music that Tom Hall mastered so well. So my own more serious musical education about blues started with a white blues traditionalist from Missouri. The story depicts some of the twists and turns that this music from the 1920s and 1930s has taken from its places of origin in the Mississippi Delta and Texas. While still in St. Louis in the 1980s I learned a few country blues songs, but I went on to pursue other musical interests, always hoping to find the time to devote to traditional country blues. The covid pandemic provided the opportunity to finally take this up—to learn both the music I loved and more about the lives of those who produced it. This book and the album that accompanies it came out of the experience.

The record accompanying this book was made with the encouragement as well as the producing and musical talents of Jack Shawde of Nashville, Tennessee. It features songs of Delta and Texas bluesmen and one song written by a female blues artist. I discuss each of the songs on the album in this book, as well as the artists famous for performing them. Those songs and artists are:

- "Backwater Blues" by Bessie Smith
- "Love in Vain" by Robert Johnson
- "Big Road Blues" by Tommy Johnson
- "Pay Day" by Mississippi John Hurt
- "Devil Got My Woman" by Skip James
- "Hard Time Killing Floor Blues" by Skip James
- "Catfish Blues" by Robert Petway
- "Shinin' Moon" by Lightnin' Hopkins

The song arrangements on the album honor the traditional recordings without attempting to duplicate them exactly. For my part, I learned acoustic guitar versions of the songs. In various places I slightly amended lyrics for my own purposes, true to the spirit of the blues artists. I then recorded vocals and guitars and sent these versions of the songs to Jack, who sprinkled magic dust on them in his Nashville studio. Jack did most of the arrangements, sending me versions to listen to during the process. He also occasionally drew on the talent of others in his musical circles. Thanks are due to Diane Ward, Bob Taylor, and Frank Tedesco, all of whom contributed to the album. Thanks is also due to Looch at Miami Beach Recording Studios for engineering and mastering the record.

In the book I provide short biographies of the artists whose music is recorded on the album, drawing attention to some themes especially in religion and politics that are relevant to the blues of these artists. The book is framed through my lens as a professional philosopher. However, the point of this book is not to offer a detailed historical overview of each musician's life or an outline of what each of these musicians believed—to provide, if you will, their respective "philosophies of life." I do though sketch the lives of these artists with philosophical issues as formative background interests.

*Portraits of the Blues* was written at the suggestion of Don Sarley of Arco Records in Miami, who proposed writing it to accompany the record. Irena Gapkovska, a Macedonian artist who now lives between Perpignan, France and Skopje, Macedonia agreed to do portraits for the book, and the book owes much to her outstanding artwork. Various other individuals have contributed in important ways to this work. Marty Bussey copyedited an early version of the manuscript. Nicholas Thaw made valuable suggestions about the development of the project. Special debts of gratitude are owed to Sarah Jacob and Rose Gargiulo. Sarah was a vital interlocutor during the entire project. Over the course of a couple years while working on this book, I've discussed all the details of it with her, and she's read the manuscript at each of its stages, making invaluable comments. The book would not be in its present form without her amazing support. Rose Gargiulo of Imagine Media Concepts not only formatted the book and designed the CD and book covers, but she also served as a publishing consultant. Her help has been enormous.

The love of country blues that is shared by those who influenced and became involved in this project attests again to the fact that from places like Avalon and Breton, Mississippi, country blues traveled to St. Louis, Miami, Nashville, and Perpignan, France. The blues has made a voyage now over a century long and leaving enthusiasts in all nations in its wake. The project is a tribute to the music and the musicians who created the original songs loved by those of us involved in this endeavor. We have ended up with a unique multi-media presentation of the blues.

We hope you enjoy it!

# Chapter 1: Introduction

Blues music is distinctly American. Its roots are embedded in the black sorrow songs, hollers, and spirituals, merging with white, southern folk music. Blues originated among African Americans as a transcultural phenomenon—emergent from the African traditions transplanted into a soil not only affected by the new musical styles, but also by the pathological cruelty embodied in systems of racial injustice. "Blues" is unique as a musical genre in designating not only a musical style but also an emotional state of sorrow. The latter, as embodied in the music, is in my view expressive of the universal suffering of human life—but it was born of a particular sorrow, the afflictions of African Americans in the United States.

One often noted testament to this music being of African American rather than African origin is that the blues does not emerge in any of the other cultures that had enslaved peoples of Africa. It doesn't emerge in Haiti or Jamaica or anywhere else in the Caribbean. It emerges as a product of forces at play in the United States. The African Americans who created the blues had been in the United States for many generations. In contrast to various areas of the Caribbean that long continued the slave trade with Africa, continually bringing new generations of Africans to their soils, enslavement in the US became more thoroughly intergenerational. And many of the African cultural influences that remained among African

Americans were augmented under the dominant cultural influences of the United States.

Blues music doesn't have a linear origin. Elements contributing to its development are the musical traditions of Africa, mixed with influences of music and instruments of Scotland and Ireland, the experience of oppression during the U.S. enslavement period, the failed efforts of the Reconstruction era and the extreme repression of the Jim Crow South. We can look to music-internal influences on the form. Something musically in blues differed enough from earlier folk forms to warrant calling it a new genre. But the designation is anything but straightforward. It comes to be primarily identified with a 12 bar or 16 bar form, with blue and sliding notes, with a tendency to have two repeated lines followed by a third divergent one (the famous A-A-B pattern). Robert Johnson's lyrics in "Walkin' Blues" provide one well-known example of the standard lyrical form: "You can call the blues anything you please" (2x), "But the blues ain't nothing but a doggone heart disease."[11] Yet, while Johnson's song and many other blues songs follow this lyrical pattern and have other elements characteristic of the blues genre, many famous blues songs do not do this or share other of the typical features. So while the music-internal elements are important for describing the blues, they are not all necessary parts of the genre designation. Rather, songs have some combination of these features. How many and which specific ones are necessary? That proves hard to say precisely.

We can also look to technologies to understand the origin of the blues: the type of instruments that were developed, like the blues harp and the guitar that came to dominate early blues or the later electric amps and microphones, which influenced the direction of the art form. Similarly, we might look to the formatting requirement dictated by the recording technologies, which resulted in demand for songs of about three minutes in length, the length that the major recording technology allowed. This came to be replicated in the radio format. So 18 minute songs known from Charlie Patton's early work became rarer, and three minute songs like Robert Johnson's became more common. Also key were decisions by the music industry in the 1920s to produce music that was marketed to particular races. In their "race catalogues," labels like Okeh and Paramount marketed blues to African Americans. Hillbilly music by contrast was marketed to white rural folk. These economic decisions helped cement demands and erect a starker barrier between music genres where previously, at least for a time, there had been less of one.

Another factor that influenced blues becoming what it became was the oppression of the "blues people" from whom this folk music emerged. The themes of early blues are the themes of particular importance in black America, with an emphasis on wandering, one of the great freedoms that distinguished the lives of African Americans in the postbellum South from their lives in the period before that. Other topics are economic hardship, especially acute in the community producing this music, and which became even more extreme in the Depression. Of course, some common themes reverberate throughout white rural music as well: lost love, jealousy, infidelity, sensuality, loneliness. More unique to blues are songs about the blues itself, as well as scattered references to hoodoo in a music genre that becomes known by many as the "devil's music."

Blues comes into existence as an aggregate of numerous factors. It becomes defined by a characteristic form, but also by the themes of the lyrics. In its earliest period it comes to be largely identified with black Americans. And as already noted, "blues" designates more than a musical form. The term "blues" or "blue devils" had described deep sadness since the 17th century in Europe. The term, used in reference to music, evokes the emotion. More than any other musical genre, blues becomes associated with the expression of a particular emotion.

Yet blues music does not only express the emotional "blues": It becomes a means for working through or exorcising the blue emotions. Blues artists continually speak and sing of having the blues and of their desire to get rid of the blues. The music is experienced by many of its players and its audience alike as a means to sort through the troubles of life. Enjoyment of the blues becomes a kind of musical therapy. Sometimes the blues are thought to be existential, part of the general human experience. Sometimes they are identified as more particular to the black American experience of those who originated the genre.

Blues in the meantime is acknowledged as one of the premiere cultural contributions of African Americans—or anyone else—to the 20th century. It was however slow to gain this recognition. Among the early 20th century U.S. black and white churchgoers, it was often shunned as "the devil's music." Among a majority of early 20th century intellectuals, it was thought too primitive of an expression of art to deserve our attention. Even black middle-class intellectuals of the early 20th century generally thought it was too crude and raw to fulfill the political role that the many of these intellectuals believed great African American art should fulfill—of leading white America to see the humanity of its racially oppressed minority population.

Nonetheless, the blues made its way from a black subculture of the country and the original race labels of the 1920s into mainstream American culture—in ways the intellectuals of the time had not anticipated. Country blues went on to influence urban electric blues, rhythm and blues, soul, and rock music. The countrified versions were also "rediscovered" during the blues revival of the 1960s, where the music gained a political salience in this movement, as many of the aficionados took it up in part as a stance against the tradition of racism that has been such a strong undercurrent in American society. Though blues did not so often have an explicit political message, it nonetheless became a political music, demonstrating that the meaning of an art form is not limited by the intensions of its creators.

Blues has become a part of our universal cultural inheritance. In this book, I honor that inheritance, offering portraits of artists who have influenced my own recent foray into country blues music and who feature on my album. *Portraits of the Blues* is written to accompany that album. In the book I intermix biographical overviews of the artists featured on the record with hints of philosophical and socio-cultural themes relevant to the artists' lives and work as well as the broader reception of blues.

The portraits that follow speak to the context of the origin of the music of these artists. Typical themes in the biographical portraits include the religious views of the artists or portrayed in the songs they wrote or performed. Sometimes the book highlights political stances. Now and again it touches on the question: What is the blues?

## Endnotes

[1] From Robert Johnson's version of "Walkin' Blues," Vocalion, 1936. In this version, Johnson adds lyrics differing from Son House's original 1930 version of the song.

# Chapter 2: Bessie Smith

(circa April 15, 1894 - Sept. 26,1937)

On September 26, 1937, driving from Memphis toward Clarksdale, Mississippi, on Highway 61, Bessie Smith had a horrible car accident that led to fatal injuries. The "Empress of Blues," as she had come to be known, met her end near the birthplace of Son House in the region that more than any would become identified as the birthplace of the blues.

In light of Smith's death, John Hammond, the well-known record producer and publicist, who had produced Smith's last album and was producing his famous "From Spiritual to Swing Concert" at Carnegie Hall, dedicated the concert to her honor. Hammond became famous early in his career for producing black artists, from Bessie Smith to Billie Holiday, and he was instrumental in convincing Bennie Goodman to play and record with racially integrated bands. In his view drawing attention to black American music was a vital means to help overcome America's racism. As he said: "To bring recognition to the Negro's supremacy in jazz [and we can add, other American music] was the most effective and constructive form of social protest I could think of."[1] The Carnegie Hall concert featured not only the music of jazz legends, but that of Son House, Lead Belly and other country blues stars. It also spotlighted phonograph recordings of Robert Johnson, who Hammond had hoped to secure for the show but who had died shortly before the performance.

The story of Bessie Smith's death that Hammond told at the Carnegie Hall concert underscored the racial injustice in the country that Hammond hoped attention to blues and jazz might address. As Hammond said:

> We are dedicating the program to Bessie Smith, who personifies the grandeur and warmth of Negro music. Bessie Smith was seriously injured in an auto accident in Virginia fourteen months ago. Taken to a hospital, she was denied admittance because she was a Negro. Before she could be taken to the proper hospital she was dead. In this story you have an example of the cruelties Negro musicians share with their fourteen million brothers in America.[2]

The story was disturbing, sad, somehow unsurprising, but it was also untrue—on numerous counts. Smith had died in Mississippi, not Virginia. More importantly, she was not turned away from a hospital because of race. Smith was admitted to the first hospital she arrived at, but there was nothing that could be done. She died of the results of injuries sustained in the late-night car wreck. Nonetheless, the myth of this injustice spread. Given the history and pervasiveness of racism, it was simply all too believable, even if it was false.

Bessie Smith had been the most successful blues artist of the 1920s. The story of her cause of death, though a lie, did contain truth as embodied in myth: What made the narrative compelling for a storyteller like Hammond was that Smith had lived through a period of extreme racial hatred. She may not have died because of this injustice, but she easily could have. And the music that she gifted the world narrates the experiences created in large part from the conditions of life so strongly influenced by the cruel circumstances Smith and many who wrote songs with her had endured under Jim Crow laws. That experience had created a situation in which it was commonplace for black Americans to experience the kinds of realities related in Hammond's tale.

Smith's lifework in part resonated with her fans because it gave voice to the daily struggles and pain of many African Americans in the South, against the backdrop of the legislation and ethos of Jim Crow. In this context, Smith's life and music took on political dimensions, even in cases when that may not have been part of her intention. In her broad career Smith did sing and write numerous songs that are explicitly political. However, most of her music did not explicitly take up politics. Nonetheless, by expressing the sensibilities, trials and tribulations of her community, Smith's music served the ends of community building. It was thus political in a broad sense, as appreciated by contemporary scholars of African American Studies like Angela Davis or Cornel West and as was appreciated by her one-time producer, Hammond, more than by most of Smith's contemporaries.

Most of the Black intellectuals of Smith's time under-appreciated her political importance. This is in particular true of those associated with the most important early 20th century African American intellectual movement, the Harlem

Renaissance. These thinkers also tended to under-appreciate the country blues musicians highlighted in this book.

The most important of the old guard thinkers of this movement were W.E.B. Du Bois and Alain Locke.[3] Du Bois was the first African American to receive a Ph.D. from Harvard. Locke was the first black American to receive a Rhodes scholarship. Both went on to become influential educators for generations of African Americans, Du Bois as a professor at Atlanta University and one of the founders of the NAACP, Locke as a professor at Howard University. Both thinkers early on underlined that African American art could be leveraged politically. Indeed, they developed ideas like those Hammond eventually adopted, arguing that the black contribution to American and world culture had the potential to lead Americans to revise their distorted views of the inferiority of African Americans. Both thinkers optimistically thought that white Americans who were exposed to the virtuosity of black artistic creations would revise their false racist notions and recognize the dignity of black Americans.

In contrast to Hammond, however, both Du Bois and Locke tended to highlight high art. Both thinkers argued that black artists could create art on par with the greatest art of Europe. Locke, more than Du Bois, underlined that the African Americans would need to plumb the depths of their specific heritage to create art with universal appeal. But high art was the focus of both men. While later in his life, Locke became more appreciative of the blues as a unique African American cultural expression, he remained somewhat restrained in his support. Locke pleaded for African American art, drawing on the particularities of African American experience, that "balanced excellence with social consciousness."[4] But there seemed a remaining concern that blues too directly challenged important elements of the prevailing moral system.

This concern was stronger still in Du Bois. Du Bois subsumed the goal of art to that of politics. As he infamously said, "All art is propaganda."[5] In alignment with his political functionalism, he underlined the need for black artists to lead impeccable moral lives, since the example of these artists would influence the public view of all black Americans. Smith's music, raunchy and guttery, was not projecting the image of black America that Du Bois thought was needed to facilitate political change.

Elain Feinstein, one of Smith's biographers, notes a view aligning with that of Du Bois that most of the intellectuals of the Harlem Renaissance would have applied to Smith and more generally to the country blues artists: "Successful blacks disliked Bessie, because they felt her behaviour endangered their own image of themselves."[6] It—like the behavior of the later country blues artists—embodied too much the widespread stereotypical behavior that whites attributed to blacks.

Nonetheless, in ways too little appreciated by the old guard of the Harlem Renaissance, Smith's music, like that of the country blues artists discussed later in this book, provided a sense of pride and a sense of belonging to many who heard their own concerns expressed in that music. In finding a voice so expressive of parts of their own realities, many came to feel their own identities and their own worth affirmed. Smith's voice, like the voice of the country blues players, gave them voice in some important sense. In these ways Smith's music and the music of country blues artists took on political meaning even when this was not its expressed purpose.

Smith was born in Chattanooga, Tennessee, likely on April 15, 1894, the date noted on her marriage application. But as is the case with so many Southern black Americans from her period, the records are not entirely reliable. By the time Bessie was nine years old, both of her parents had passed away. She was then raised by her eldest sister, Viola.[2] As a child she performed on street corners with her older brother, Clarence. But in 1912 she was hired by the Moses Stokes company where her older brother Clarence had begun working as a comedian and master of ceremonies in 1910 or 1911 and where Bessie met Ma Rainey. It's not known how long Bessie stayed with the company, where she initially was hired as a dancer. However, Thomas A. Dorsey recounts that in the minstrel world Bessie was "already a star in her own right" by around 1913 or 1914.[8]

Though stories are prevalent of Bessie's tutelage under Ma Rainey, Rainey didn't teach Bessie to sing. She did, though, serve as a model of a successful blues singer and entertainer, and the two women did develop a professional friendship. Bessie's biographer, Chris Albertson, relates the largest of the myths, about which the two stars on at least one occasion shared a laugh—namely, that Rainey had in fact kidnapped the young Bessie and forced her to perform as part of her and her husband's minstrel show.[9] The tale was absurd. Bessie in any case would surely have needed no kidnapping. She was longing for work on the road from the time she was a child.

The minstrel show circuit served as a training ground for Smith as for the other early blues divas. It provided the venue in which she was able to develop her skills as an entertainer and singer. Rainey's blues did serve as a model for Smith. They were a link to the blues tradition that was being cultivated by lone guitarists on the street corners and at train stations throughout the South.[10] The minstrel circuit was also a path to a more lucrative career for a talented young woman. In her early minstrel show days, Smith was earning ten dollars per week (around $320 in 2024 currency), but it was said that stagehands would also regularly pick up three or four dollars in tips for her that were thrown at the stage during her performances (around $100 to $125 in 2024). This is considerably more than she would have otherwise been earning as a teenager; and she was acquiring the skills for her later economic success.[11] Smith's performances throughout her life always bore the mark of her early minstrel show training. Even the fierce projection of her voice witnesses to the roots of her artistry in this show setting, where there were no microphones.

Though she honed her craft on the minstrel circuit, it was with the advent of the recording industry's focus on female blues singers that Smith later reached her zenith. Popular vocal music of white artists had been recorded in the 1910s. But

Mamie Smith was the first black vaudeville singer to record a vocal blues song. Her recording of "Crazy Blues" in 1920 sold 75,000 copies within the first month of being recorded. It was important, along with earlier blues numbers like W.C. Handy's "St. Louis Blues," in beginning to define the blues genre.[12] One other result of the success of the song was that it reinforced the decision of many other record labels to offer catalogues of black music and their concomitant search for new black, especially female, recording stars. In 1923 Bessie was first able to record, performing a song for Columbia Records. Her version of "Down Hearted Blues" sold 780,000 copies within six months of its release.[13] Her recording career was launched.

In this early period, even despite her success in traveling tent shows, Southerners generally were reluctant to book her into the mainstream theaters. In the North she was largely booked in black venues.[14]

Part of the reservations about Smith had to do with her bawdy stage persona and bawdy personality. In her songs and her life she encapsulated the stereotype of a blues singer. In the words of Chris Albertson, she embodied the blues archetype "as a big fat mama who drank a lot, fought like a dog, and sang like an angel."[15] The same characteristics that won her fans and praise also brought skepticism from, if not the disdain of, many of the African American churchgoers and the African American East Coast intellectuals.

Black Swan Records, a black owned record label, turned her down for a record contract. The label, which had a short run from 1921 to 1923, was founded by a former student of Du Bois, Harry Price, with the expressed object of creating music that would feature the genius of African American artists. One goal of the label was to produce music that moved beyond African American stereotypes. So, for example, it produced classical recordings of the soprano, Revella Hughes. Yet it also did produce blues, and their greatest recording star was Ethel Waters.

Turning away Smith was of course a business folly. But Black Swan found Smith's manner too crass and rude. For Price, like the old guard black intellectuals of the Harlem Renaissance who inspired him, Smith embodied too much of the moral degradation and traditional black stereotypes that they wanted black artists to overcome.[16]

Smith's first hit, "Down Home Blues," was raunchy. Her self-assured attitude and sexual liberation are politically refreshing to many today, but they were enjoyed with less openness—if at all—three years after women had gained the right to vote in the United States. The sexual innuendos in this work were blatant: "I got the world in a jug, the stopper's in my hand (2x), I'm gonna hold it until you men come under my command."[17] Other hits, like "Need a Little Sugar in My Bowl," were similarly provocative.[18] The rhyme to the title line of that song was: "Need a little hotdog between my rolls." Such analogies were in fact too direct to be more than privately enjoyed in a period of widespread moral prudery.

For much of the black middle class, the problems were not just with Smith's stage persona. She also exuded the coarseness of the blues in the way she lived her life: She drank corn liquor and was known for reaching inside her dress to pull out change of up to a thousand dollars, which she carried around with her. She had numerous tuffs with women, beating her long-time friend, Ruby Walker, more than once. She also fought with men and epitomized pugnacious toughness. In 1925, she was stabbed by a man after a concert, but still chased the male assailant down the street for three blocks with the knife sticking in her side before collapsing. As Albert notes, though the assault had occurred at four o'clock in the morning, she still showed up for her afternoon concert.[19] Does anything express the stereotypical spirit of the blues more than this?

Though Smith exemplified an image of the blues that contributed to its poor reputation among churchgoers, her own attitude toward religion was anything but hostile. In spite of Smith's roughness and toughness, she did not eschew traditional religion, like those who considered blues the devil's music would have supposed. She instead expressed a rather more complicated relationship to religion. As Albertson, notes, there were times when Smith "faced hard times with hard liquor and hope,"[20] singing songs about the devil and fully embracing what many perceived as blasphemous. Nonetheless, throughout her life she also expressed a religious sensibility. As Maud Smith, the widow of her brother Clarence, noted:

"In every town that we would get in, if we got in on a Sunday morning early enough, we'd all go to church."[21] Maud also recounted that "Bessie could sing some of the most beautiful church hymns, and she often did that around the house." Her occasional drummer Zutty Singleton, also underlined Smith's spirituality: "She was real close to God, very religious."

The style of her performance shared some broad similarities to church music as well. As Singleton also recalled, "She always mentioned the Lord's name. That's why her blues seemed almost like hymns."[22] Various commentators, like the guitar player Danny Barker, similarly noted a resemblance between her music and church music. But Barker also highlighted her ability, similar to the best preachers, to hold people spellbound: "You would recognize a similarity between what she was doing and what those preachers and evangelists from there did, and how they moved people. Bessie did the same thing on stage. She, in a sense, was like people like Billy Graham are today. Bessie was in a class with those people. She could bring about mass hypnotism."[23]

Thematically, Smith's repertoire covered a wide gamut of topics. Though she embodied many of the ideals of blues and can be said to have sung from experience, she was an entertainer, adopting multiple perspectives on a topic, assuming roles. Singing about a particular perspective did not mean she agreed with it. Indeed, in her songs she assumed the viewpoints of too many diverse and contradictory figures for that to be the case.

She sang of spousal abuse, of affairs, of murders, of women leaving their men and heading down the road. Smith lived as fearlessly and roughly as many of the characters of her songs. In her outstanding book, *Blues Legacies and Black Feminism: Gertrude "Ma" Rainey, Bessie Smith, and Billie Holiday*, Angela Davis highlights the political elements of the female blues singers with a focus on Smith. One of the keys to understanding the politics of Smith, as well as Rainey and some other women blues singers, is to grasp how their music created community. It served this function especially among black women, as it often expressed a shared trauma. For these blues women, the personal was political; and the personal was tied to community. Stylistically many of the female blues artists open with lines to create community. The opening of "I Used to Be Your Sweet Mama" provides a good example. As Smith begins the song, she invokes a women's community: "All you women understand, what it is to be in love with a two-time man."[24]

Smith calls out to the community of women she is singing to about a familiar plight. The story continues as a standard advice song. She will not passively tolerate her man's infidelity. Instead, she sings in the past tense of how, given her man's infidelity, she *used to be* his sweet woman. But because he "proved unfaithful," she will from here on out be "mean and hateful." The heroine of this song is doing anything but passively accepting her circumstances.

The women Smith portrays are not traditional passive subjects, but active protagonists, seizing their own fates. They are both sexually and physically aggressive, and their stories give voice to many of the common themes of women who were Smith's fans.

Smith does sing some songs about more clear social themes. Examples include "Working Women Blues" about the poor labor conditions of black women, and "Poor Man's Blues" about general issues of economic disparity. Her "Backwater Blues," featured on the accompanying album, highlights another social issue—namely, how the devastating Delta floods of the 1920s and 1930s crushed the lives of many who were already living precariously. Smith decided to write her song in Spring of 1927 after an experience outside a Southern Ohio town. While Smith was on the way to a concert, her train had to be stopped. The train tracks had been covered by water from a flood, and the band had to be taken to the concert by row boat. When the audience asked her to play a blues about the flood, she regretted to tell them she could not because she did not know one. But after the concert she went home and wrote "Backwater Blues."[25] The publication of the song came with the cataclysmic 1927 Mississippi Delta flood, a horrible event, though one that extremely boosted the sales of her record. As Smith sings in that song:

*When it rains five days*
*And the skies turn dark as night (2x)*
*Then trouble's takin' place*
*In the lowlands at night*

*I woke up this morning',*
*Can't even get out of my door (2x)*
*That's enough trouble*
*To make a poor girl wonder where she wanna go*

*They rowed a little boat*
*About five miles 'cross the pond (2x)*
*I packed all my clothes,*
*Throwed "em in and they rowed me along*

*When it thunders and lightnin'*
*And the wind begins to blow (2x)*
*There's thousands of people*
*Ain't got no place to go*

*I went and stood upon*
*some high old lonesome hill (2x)*
*Then looked down on the house*
*Where I used to live*

*Back Water Blues*
*Caused me to pack my things and go (2x)*
*Cause my house fell down,*
*And I can't live there no mo'*

For those whose lives were already on the margin, floods and other unexpected events sent them into absolute destitution. The 1927 floods that coincided with Smith's release of the song resulted in over 600,000 people losing their homes, with some appraisals being as high as 930,000.[26] The National Safety Council estimates that a thousand people died in the Yazoo-Mississippi Delta.[27] Davis provides thorough background context for understanding the impact the song would have had.

Though floods seemed to be acts of God, black communities were often given the overflow of water to take the pressure off the levee systems. These African American communities were also in precarious living arrangements and jobs, which meant that such acts took a worse toll on them than on others (as such events regrettably still do). In the 1927 floods, government aid did in fact go to white families, but black Americans were forced to pay for food and other necessities. This forced many to take loans from plantation owners, once again becoming indebted or further indebted.[28]

As Davis, notes, "Will Percy, the head of the food relief program in Greenville, Mississippi, announced that 'no able-bodied negro is entitled to be fed at all unless he is tagged as a laborer.'"[29] Similar restrictions applied to women and children. As Davis quotes from the report:

> No rations will be issued to Greenville negro women and children unless there is no man in the family, which fact must be certified by a white person.

> No negro man in Greenville nor their families will be rationed unless the men join the labor gang or are employed.

> Negro men...drawing a higher wage [than $1. a day] are not entitled to be rationed.[30]

Smith's song is not an explicit call for political action. However, it clearly relates a situation understood at the time as particularly weighing on the black residents of the Delta. It was generally understood that some suffered worse from such natural disasters than others, and as was often the case, there was increased police surveillance of activity of the African American community during such times of crisis.

Davis' assessment is "Songs like 'Backwater Blues' are much more than the folk history to which they are often relegated. Transforming individual emotions into collective responses to adversity, they transcend the particular circumstances that inspired them and become metaphors about oppression."[31]

While race labels in the early 1920s had already started producing some music of country roots, and among archivists and intellectuals there was an attempt to find the real roots of blues music in country blues players, Smith in this period had a very successful recording career as a blues singer. Columbia had marketed her as "Queen of the Blues." She became its Empress. Not counting later re-releases, Smith is thought to have sold between six and ten million records by the time she ended her recording career.[32] In her time, she was America's biggest blues star.

Smith made one of the strongest contributions of any artist of the early 20th century to American culture. Over the arc of history, her artistry did a good part of what the major African American aestheticians of the Harlem Renaissance, like Du Bois and Locke, thought great African American art should do. Carl Van Vechten, an influential writer for the New York Times, who did much to promote blues music, had written of one 1926 performance, Smith "sings blues as they are understood and admired by the coloured masses."[33] Though the songs that pleased the masses were not projecting the image black intellectuals thought was needed, in the end these had enormous cultural and even political effects.

Later blues enthusiasts, especially those looking for the roots of the music in the country sounds, classified Smith's "vaudeville blues" as an offshoot of a more genuine expression of the genre. But her minstrel show roots place her squarely at the origin of the genre. Her "bluesy" attitude also embodies the common stereotype of the genre as well as anyone's. Blues musicians of all varieties have also continued to come back to her music, even if they have rearranged it to their own less vaudeville styles. Lightnin' Hopkins, an early electric blues pioneer who also became a major figure in the 1960s country blues revival, recorded numerous songs of Smith. Among those is "Backwater Blues," which he retitled "That Mean Old Twister." Hopkins arranged the song for guitar and added many lyrics. The rhythm guitar on the recording of that song on the album accompanying this book is indebted to Hopkins' arrangement.

Billie Holiday cited Smith's influence and recorded "Tain't Nobody's Business if I Do," a song made popular by Smith. The 1958 recordings "Dinah Washington Sings Bessie Smith" and "LaVene Baker Sings Bessie Smith" demonstrate the continued resonance of her music for that generation. Maureen Mahon also points out that in the 1940s Mama Thorton was billed as "Bessie Smith's Little Sister." Thorton's Smith-style vocals and music went on to influence Janis Joplin, who recorded a version of Thorton's "Ball and Chain," and even Elvis, who recorded Thorton's "Hound Dog."[34]

Blues was already in transition when Smith passed away. After the rise of the blues divas, race record labels and archivists trying to preserve America's folk music began a search for the roots of the blues genre. They looked to country blues musicians known from street corners and train stations throughout the South. Though nowhere as successful as Smith in their lifetimes, these country blues musicians—to whom the rest of this volume is devoted—also went on to have enormous influence on the development of 20th century popular music. Soul, funk, and rhythm and blues all have roots in this music, as does British and American rock. We see the influence of especially the country blues players on Eric Clapton, Jimmy Page, the Rolling Stones, the Butterfield Blues band, Stevie Ray Vaughan, and George Thorogood to name just some obvious examples.

The musical ripple effects of country blues have been enormous. Ironically, the political effects of that music—like Smith's—have also been significant. Though few of the country blues musicians from the 1920s to the 1950s had explicit political intentions, their music nonetheless went on to have positive political impacts, as it was taken up by students in the blues revival of the 1960s who often were very explicit about the political importance of the music and the musicians who created it in challenging a tradition of racist politics.

## Endnotes

[1] Qtd. in Dunstan Prial, 2006. *The Producer. John Hammond and the Soul of American Music* (New York: Farrar, Straus and Giroux), 117.

[2] Prial, 117 ff.

[3] For Pulitzer Prize winning biographies of these intellectuals, see David Levering Lewis, *W.E.B. Du Bois. A Biography* (New York: Henrey Holt, 2009); Jeffrey C. Stewart, *The New Negro. The Life of Alain Locke* (Oxford: Oxford UP, 2018).

[4] W.E.B. Du Bois, Criteria of Negro Art. *The Crisis*, 32(6), 1926, 290-297.

[5] See Richard Keaveny, "Aesthetics and the Issue of Identity," in *The Critical Pragmatism of Alain Locke*, edited by Leonard Harris (Latham, Maryland: Roman & Littlefield, 1999), 135. Cp. Steven C. Tracy, 2001, *Langston Hughes and the Blues* (Chicago: University of Illinois Press), 26ff.

[6] As Davis underlines, Elain Feinstein saw part of the reason for the condemnation of Smith as related to what Amiri Baraka saw as informing much of the African American rejection of blues in general. The mores of the blues artists didn't respect the hierarchy within the black community between middle class blacks and poor rural ones. Taking Feinstein's words about Smith, but applying them more generally: The more profane of the blues artists were "refusing to acknowledge the class system the blacks had set up which put the white world at the unreachable top of the tree" Davis, 154. See also Amiri Baraka, *Blues People. Negro Music in White America* (New York: Harper, 1999), 124ff.

[7] Chris Albertson, Bessie (New Haven: Yale UP, 2003), 1-8.

[8] Albertson, 15.

[9] Albertson, 14ff.

[10] Albertson, 12.

[11] Albertson, 14. This story is related by Leigh Whipper, who may have been exaggerating or in any case wrong about the details. He relates that Smith's best received song from 1913 was "Weary Blues." But that song wasn't published until 1915; and though she might have sang the song before publication, it's also odd that, if this had been her early show stopper, she never recorded the song herself.

[12] Giles Oakley, *The Devil's Music. A History of the Blues*, 2nd ed. (London: Da Capo Press, 1983).

[13] Albertson, 38.

[14] Albertson, 66.

[15] Albertson, 55.

[16] See Paul Slade, *Black Swan Blues: The Hard Rise and Brutal Fall of America's First Black-owned Record Label* (Planetslade.com, 2021).

[17] Alberta Hunter and Love Austin, "Downhearted Blues." Paramount. 1922. Smith's version was issued with Columbia A3844, Feb. 17, 1923.

[18] Williams, D. Small, and T. Brymn, Need a Little Sugar in My Bowl. Issued with Columbia, 1931.

[19] Albertson, 93.

[20] Albertson, 252.

[21] Albertson, 154.

[22] Albertson, 154ff.

[23] Albertson, 155.

[24] Bessie Smith, "I Used to Be Your Sweet Mama," Columbia 14292 D, Feb. 9, 1928.

[25] Bessie Smith, "Backwater Blues," Columbia 14159D, Feb 17, 1927. The basic guitar arrangement for the version on the recording leans on Lightnin' Hopkins rendition of the song, retitled "That Mean Old Twister," 1946, Aladdin 168. Hopkins changes numerous of the lyrics.

[26] See Phil Ratcliffe, Mississippi John Hurt. His Live his Times, His Blues (Jackson: University of Mississippi Press, 2011), 54.

[27] See Ratcliffe, 55.

[28]Angela Davis, *Blues Legacies and Black Feminism: Gertrude: Ma Rainey, Bessie Smith and Billie Holiday* (New York: Vintage Books, 1998), 109.

[29] Davis, 110.

[30] Qtd in Davis, 110.

[31] Davis, 111.

[32] Lawrence W. Levine, B*lack Culture and Black Consciousness. Afro-American Folk Thought From Slavery to Freedom* (Oxford: Oxford UP, 2007), 226.

[33] Qtd in Tracy, 94.

[34] Maureen Mahan, "How Bessie Smith Influenced a Century of Blues Music," National Public Radio, https://www.npr.org/2019/08/05/747738120/how-bessie-smith-influenced-a-century-of-popular-music, accessed July 17, 2023.

# Chapter 3: Robert Johnson

(May 8, 1911 - Aug. 16, 1938)

Robert Johnson's "body was wrapped in a white linen sheet and placed in the skinny wooden boxes that were used as coffins for indigents." So runs the story of Johnson's burial by Ruth Eskridge, whose husband was contacted to dig his grave: "Brought it up here—slid it off and come on back. In them days they buried you the same day you died. Wudn't no way to keep a body like today. It would start smellin'."[1]

Robert Johnson, the man said to have sold his soul to the devil, was given a Christian burial of sorts: Reverend Starks, a jackleg preacher with no ordination or education but who provided services for trade, officiated the ceremony, putting Johnson to rest in a small cemetery next to Little Zion Church in Greenwood, Mississippi. Johnson's family, after learning of his death and his pauper's burial, had the body exhumed, put in a proper casket, and returned to the same grave. That was the end of the life of Robert Johnson, the man. However, the myths about his life and death had already started, and they would live on like few others.

As in the case of Bessie Smith, John Hammond again was instrumental in spreading misinformation about Johnson's death. About four months after Johnson died, at Hammond's "From Spirituals to Swing" concert at Carnegie Hall, Hammond told the audience: "Robert Johnson died last week at the precise moment when Vocalion scouts finally reached him and told him that he was booked to appear at Carnegie Hall on December 23."[2] Hammond made up significant details. Hammond had been enthralled with Johnson and had scouts looking for him. However, they found he had recently died. The death certificate was filed August 18, 1938. Johnson was 26 years of age.[3]

Johnson lived in the midst of the Delta blues musical developments as a transitional figure. Born in Hazlehurst, Mississippi, about May 8, 1911, he moved with his mother to Memphis for the first part of his youth. But his youth, like the rest of his life, was marked by movement—a movement that eventually afforded him contact with various blues musical styles that he was able to synthesize.

Johnson's lifelong devotion to playing guitar and his traveling to different regions to do so was key to his musical development, though in the popular cultural myth his musical genius was attributed to nefarious forces. Son House, an established musician who played in Johnson's stead at the "From Spirituals to Swing" concert, told one of the key stories that led many to believe that a Faustian bargain was the root of Johnson's guitar skills. In House's story, he first met Johnson as a "boy" who would blow a little harmonica but mostly make noise on the guitar. Johnson would regularly come to Saturday night shows where House and Willie Brown played in Robinsonville, Mississippi. Johnson would watch the guitarists attentively; and when they went on break he would get their instruments and try to play. But people regularly complained about the noise Johnson made on the instrument and asked House and Brown to take the instrument from the boy.

Though in the common depiction of this story House complains about the young Johnson's playing, House also claims to have nonetheless taught Johnson a few things on the guitar. He also recounts that Johnson went away for a few months before coming back as the guitar virtuoso we know. Depicting the first time he heard Johnson after his return from Hazlehurst, House says, "When he finished, all our mouths were standing open." Johnson was in fact so good that he eventually displaced House at these shows.

Though House's story is often used as the basis for speaking about Johnson's Mephistophelian pact, Bruce Conforth and Gayle Dean Wardlow, two of Johnson's most important recent biographers, maintain House never actually said that Johnson had a contract with the devil. Some of those further telling his story did. Mack McCormick, another of Johnson's premier biographers, maintains that Johnson himself spread the myth.[a]

Conforth and Wardlow show that the reality of Johnson's story differed from House's narrative in several respects. Johnson knew House when he was already a 19 year old and had worked as a musician for some time. In addition, the period between the meetings when House saw Johnson making noise and the meeting when Johnson's playing was jaw-dropping good was about a year, not just a few months. So Johnson was likely already better than House recalled when Johnson was attending his shows in Robinsonville; and as various guitarists can attest, focused work can lead to progress on the instrument—even if all searches for devils on country roads fail. Ironically, as Conforth and Wardlow point out, even House is known to have made amazing progress on the guitar within about a year of beginning to play.

In the period between the meetings of House and Johnson, Johnson left the Robinsonville area for Hazlehurst, about 250 miles away. There he sought his biological father, Noah Johnson, who Robert had hardly known as a boy. Robert didn't find his father in Hazlehurst. He did, though, befriend a formative guitar mentor, Isaiah or "Ike" Zimmerman. Zimmerman was born in 1898 and worked in road construction, playing guitar as an avocation. The young Johnson met him, being attracted to music he heard Zimmerman playing at a road construction site. The two took to one another, and Zimmerman eventually offered Johnson a place to stay. According to Zimmerman's daughter, Loretha, Johnson lived with the Zimmerman family like a family member, apparently mixed with intermittent trips to Memphis and other places to play music.[5] During that time, Zimmerman taught Johnson a lot on the guitar. According to Zimmerman family reports, Zimmerman knew lumber camps, fish fries and juke joints where people had money to spend. Zimmerman took Johnson along to these places to entertain. They would apparently also often practice at a graveyard near the Zimmerman house. Loretha recounted: "Daddy would always scare people and say he'd go pickin' the guitar and the haints would come out at the graveyard."[6] Zimmerman's grandson noted it was always about midnight.

As Loretha noted, also alluding to the crossroad reference: "They would leave and go to that cemetery.... He'd sit back there with him. He wasn't at no crossroads. [It] was just a path. There wasn't no crossroads. They went 'cross the road [laughs].' Cause you gotta go across [the] road and go to that cemetery."[2] The serious reaction to the question of the devilish contract by Zimmerman's daughter points to the real beliefs in hoodoo and the occult that served as the backdrop to the myth. In her interviews, Loretha noted, "My daddy ain't no devil," and she then emphasized the cemetery was a place where it was possible to play without disturbing neighbors.

The stories about Johnson's Faustian bargain were surely reinforced by earlier accounts of Johnson's blasphemy. Johnson's first wife, Virginia, had died when Johnson was young and out on the road playing blues. Many in Virginia's family and the community were convinced that Johnson's "devil's music" was responsible for that death. Some accounts suggest Johnson had a belief in God—at least as the cause of his own pain. Memphis Slim (John Len Chatman) expressed a view that surely has not done much to assuage the views of Johnson's blasphemy: "He was about one of the most evil men. Robert Johnson, every time he'd get drunk he'd cuss God. He'd go to cursin' God out and he could empty a house quick. 'Cause nobody wanted to be around him. They were afraid. He'd done called God some of the worst names you ever heard of. Then he'd look around and it wouldn't be nobody in there but him. Everybody said, 'Get away from the fool, 'cause God gon' strike him—and he might kill me, too.'"[8]

Johnson played on the devil myths in his music. In Johnson's repertoire, the references to the occult are clearest in "Hellhound on My Trail"[9] and "Me and the Devil Blues."[10] "Hellhound on My Trail" is a haunting song of a man cursed to a life of ramblin'. The melody draws on Skip James' "Devil Got My Woman." Johnson sings it in falsetto, creating a similar vocal style to James'. Instead of playing in James' customary D-minor tuning, though, he plays in E-minor, a technique he had evidently learned from Johnnie Temple.[11] The life of wandering, related in the song as because of "a hellhound on my trail," suggests that witchcraft is at the root of the rambling life of the song's protagonist. The song is a lamentation about forced movement. "I got to keep movin', I got to keep movin', Blues fallin' down like hail..., And the days keeps on worryin' me, There's a hellhound on my trail..."

Johnson's further story is rich with symbolism. His song references Christmas Eve and Christmas day, the day of the birth of the Christian savior. His lyrics suggest the possibility of a salvation, but the salvation the protagonist imagines is not in the church. It's from time with his "sweet rider." On the face of it, the reference is simply to a lover. However, given the reference to Christmas and veiled meanings within hoodoo, there are other interpretive possibilities. As religion scholar Albert Raboteau notes, it was a common belief that witches could leave their bodies and ride their victims. Such possessions, it was believed, might kill the cursed.[12] Against the backdrop of such beliefs, might Johnson have been speaking of such a holy or unholy possession? If so, was he speaking as an occult believer or simply making poetic reference to an occult belief? Knowing the intentions of an author is notoriously difficult. There is no clear evidence that Johnson did believe in or practice the occult. In any case, in this song, his longed for object of reprise, his rider, is also the ultimate cause for his continued movement. As his verses relate, his rider's curse ultimately ends whatever reprise he might find with her. She "sprinkled hot foot powder...around my door."

The sprinkling of foot powder was a common form of conjuring, thought to lead those subject to the curse to a life of restless wandering. The next verse of the song relates the stormy life that is coming, given that curse. Among the imagery are "wind risin" and "leaves trembling on the tree." Ironically, though the woman who sprinkled the powder causes the hellhounds, the protagonist nonetheless longs for his "little sweet woman's" company. In this song Johnson seems to hold women to be the cause of his tumult and the possible refuge from it.

In other songs, as well, Johnson references occult powers. "Cross Road Blues," or "Me and the Devil Blues" is a well-known example. Johnson recorded two versions of the song, the first in 1936, the second a year later. Lyrically the two versions convey the same basic story. The song starts with a reference to "you," referring to the devil, as we can see from the further lyrical development. "Early this morning, When you knocked upon my door, And I said hello Satan, I believe it's time to go." He further sings of he and the devil "walkin' side by side." The song's protagonist relates abusing his spouse, an act from which he derives some satisfaction. Yet he knows it won't help his greatest ill. The story's protagonist knows his end—where his body will be buried "down by the highway side" and where his "evil spirit" can continue his eternal restless journey and "get a Greyhound bus and ride." Johnson here identifies with the devil; and he expresses no compunction, no plans to conversion.

Like most of those attracted to Johnson's stories, Johnson may have viewed the stories as merely poetically moving. So, too, he may have cultivated a dark image for promotional value, like later rock bands that played on similar imagery, such Black Sabbath or Alice Cooper. Given the rough venues in which he played, where killings were underreported and not uncommon, such legends might have also protected him. Who wants to start trouble with the man who has the devil on his side? Statements by others about what Johnson said are the greatest hints to Johnson's own beliefs. Unfortunately, this doesn't get us far. While Peter Guralnick had maintained that Son House was convinced that Johnson had sold his soul to the devil, as earlier noted, Johnson's biographers Cornforth and Wardlow indicate that there is no evidence that House ever said this.[43] In the end, we simply have to admit that we don't know what was going on in Johnson's inner life.

Johnson's music clearly deals with themes of spiritual anguish, whether meant metaphorically or literally. Like so much blues, though, Johnson's material also deals with love, sex and betrayal—sometimes appealing to spiritual ideas common in the African American community, sometimes not. The lyrics also make frequent reference to violence and economic travails. It thematizes movement, ramblin'. It is at times misogynist, but it also often displays a sense of irony about machismo and expressed tenderness. In all these ways it captures what most of those who focus on country blues identify with its ethos.

Johnson's life reads like one we expect of a blues legend. His was the life of a rambler, not always by his own choice. Much of his hard luck was not of his own making. He didn't have a relationship with his biological father, Noah Johnson. As a child, Robert moved from Hazlehurst, where he was born, to Memphis, where he spent early school years—from 1913 to 1919. He was left in Memphis by his mother to live with his step-father, Charles Dodd. In 1919, his mother returned to Memphis and took Robert to Arkansas, 35 miles southwest of Memphis, to the area across the river from Robinsonville, Mississippi. His family knew violence. He moved—at times to avoid it.[14]

Johnson at times sang of violence towards women, such as in "32-20 Blues," a song he wrote leaning on the Skip James song "22-20 Blues." Here he repeats the lyric from James, singing that he will "take [his] 32-20, now, and cut [a woman] half in two."[15] But here he is taking up the trope of an earlier song, expressing the views of a character in the song. What we know from Johnson's life are more often expressed affections for women. He spoke of a deep love for his first wife, Virginia.

"When You Got a Good Friend" depicts a desire for a healthy partnership, such as he appeared to desire with her. "When you got a good friend, that will stay right by your side...Give her all of your spare time, love and treat her right."[16] In the song the protagonist sings of having regrets about mistreating his love and swears to "make right" by her. He again sings of his desire for a "close friend" in his lover. The final verse moves from the first person voice to the third person. It's not what he will do but what anyone should do who has a good friend.

Numerous of Johnson's songs are also full of anything but male bravado. "Love in Vain," also featured on the album produced to accompany this book, conveys great vulnerability.[17] It is a story similar to one that Johnson had himself experienced of an unrequited love. The lyrics relate a simple and recurrent theme of popular music. The lovestruck protagonist in the song is being left by his girlfriend. Up to the last minute he can't accept this, and he follows his lover up to the point of her departure on a train, hoping for her change of heart. Her transformation doesn't occur though. His love is in vain. This song fits into the genre of women's traveling blues. Some typical narratives in that genre are of women leaving to look for a man that had left them or to escape a man who is haunting them. Here the reason for the woman's departure is not clear. But Johnson's depiction is not of a weak woman. It is of a strong one who is making a decision about her life, even as it devastates the man who loves her.

"Phonograph Blues" is a song about male impotence.[18] It also lacks the macho vibrato often associated with blues. The song is a relationship story. The protagonist's partner, Beatrice (the name of one of the women Johnson had been in love with), has a phonograph that won't play (the double-entendre for sexual impotence). There must be a metaphysical cause—an act of evil by the protagonist or the woman. "Beatrice, she got a phonograph, and it won't say a lonesome word...What evil have I done, What evil has the poor girl done?"

The song relates that the protagonist's love has broken his "windin' chain," due to her infidelity—by giving her love to another man. The act of betrayal has caused his impotence. She has taken his love and "give it to your other man." The song continues with remembrances of former acts of lovemaking. Johnson plays up the male machismo, but only as it lives out in memory. In the present reality, none of the virility of the past is possible, because the protagonist has a rusty needle, and it just won't play. The protagonist is resilient, though, singing with conviction that it can work if his lover will just try him one more time. The song concludes with a repetition of the first verse. The situation is because of some cosmic act of wrongdoing—his or his woman's, maybe both of theirs.

The self-deprecating irony of "Phonograph Blues" is refreshing and cuts through simplistic portrayals of Johnson as a harsh, bad man. In fact, this, like numerous of Johnson's songs, depicts not the stereotypical male virility and female weakness, but a strong woman and a devastated man. The lyrics hardly seem like those of the wicked man Memphis Slim had described. They rather depict someone able to laugh at himself or generally to make fun of male pretenses.

Johnson's real life often lacked the kind of tender relationship he sang of longing for. He clearly had what the ancient Greek philosophers call *akrasia*, a split or weak will, evident when a person wants and does not want something at the same time. Johnson may have longed for the type of tender loving relationship he describes and yet not really wanted one at the same time. He would hardly be the first twenty-something year old with such sensibilities. This *akrasia* in any case does get at the dichotomy of emotions expressed in Johnson's songs. Johnson was a relatively young man, with wanderlust and a weakness for women and drink.

Unfortunately for blues lovers, Johnson's final tryst led to his untimely death. Johnson appears to have been poisoned by R.D. Davis, the husband of the woman with whom he had his last affair. The husband mixed moth balls in a drink for Johnson, a mix that didn't often lead to death, but normally only to severe suffering. Johnson though had just been diagnosed with an ulcer. Given his underlying condition, the drink was his death potion.[19]

Johnson's life and death and legend continue to excite the imagination. Certainly no blues player captured the myth of the blues for the 1960s blues rock bands quite as much as he did. He lived a rambling life of a blues man, drinking, philandering, and celebrating it in song. And in the end, the man with the alleged Faustian bargain died at the hands of a jealous husband at the young age of 26.

## Endnotes

[1] Bruce M. Conforth and Gayle Dean Wardlow, *Up Jumped the Devil. The Real Life of Robert Johnson* (Chicago: Chicago Review Press, 2019), 256.

[2] Conforth and Wardlow, 266.

[3] Conforth and Wardlow, 258.

[4] See Conforth and Wardlow, 87ff. See also Robert "Mack" McCormick, *Biography of a Phantom. A Robert Johnson Blues Odyssey* (Washington, DC: Smithsonian Books), 2023.

[5] Conforth and Wardlow, 191 ff.

[6] Conforth and Wardlow, 106.

[7] Conforth and Wardlow, 105.

[8] Conforth and Wardlow, 83.

[9] Robert Johnson, "Hellhound on My Trail," Vocalion, 1937.

[10] Robert Johnson, "Me and the Devil Blues," Vocalion, 1938.

[11] Cornforth and Wardlow, 211.

[12] Albert Raboteau, *Slave Religion* (Oxford, Oxford UP, 2004), cp. 14.

[13] Conforth and Wardlow, 5.

[14] Conforth and Wardlow, 45ff.

[15] Robert Johnson, 32-20 Blues, Vocalion, 1936.

[16] Robert Johnson, "When You Got a Good Friend," Vocalion, 1936.

[17] Robert Johnson, "Love in Vain," Vocalion, 1936.

[18] Robert Johnson, "Phonograph Blues," Vocalion, 1936.

[19] During a later investigation it was suggested he had died of syphilis. But Conforth and Wardlow highlight the vomiting and pain as well as the time of his death were well documented, providing stronger evidence of poisoning as the cause of death.

# Chapter 4: Tommy Johnson

(Jan. 1896 - Nov. 1, 1956)

L ike his 12 siblings, Tommy Johnson was born on a plantation owned by George Miller about 20 miles south of Jackson, Mississippi, near Terry.[1] Tommy was the sixth child. After all of the children had been born, the family moved to Crystal Springs. The family was related to Lonnie Johnson, one of the early great jazz and blues singers and innovators on the guitar. Most of the family on the side of Tommy's mother (the Wilsons) were also musicians, though Tommy's mother was not.[2] According to Tommy's brother, LeDell, their uncles had a band that played "jump ups" and "love songs." The older Johnson kids learned some of these songs on guitar. They mostly learned the various folk blues songs that were known in the area. LeDell claims he initially taught Tommy to play. But that ended when Tommy, at about the age of 16, around 1912, ran off with a much older woman.[3] Tommy returned two years later without the woman, but as an accomplished blues player. He had spent the time away in the Delta, near Rolling Fork and in Boyle, Mississippi, towns between around 90 and 140 miles from Crystal Springs.

While away and exposed to new music, Tommy had become an accomplished songwriter and came back playing in a style not known in the Crystal Springs area. As LeDell describes it: "Me and him would play for some white folks here, and he'd just set up and just sit there and follow with his box, and he could make a song in ten minutes."[4] The process depicted is not of Tommy playing new songs he learned but of him writing blues songs with the tools he had mastered while away. Indeed, according to David Evans, the only major biographer of Johnson, the only song Tommy played that he claimed he had learned from someone else was "Black Mare Blues," which he said he had learned from Dick Bankston.

As creative as Tommy's songs were, though, they did draw on many widely shared lyrical and musical themes— musical ideas he became instrumental in spreading. For his part, LeDell was convinced that Tommy owed his skillset to a Faustian bargain like the one many believed Robert Johnson had made. He relates the following story, which he claims his brother told him:

> If you want to learn how to play anything you want to play and learn how to make songs yourself, you take your guitar and you go to where a road crosses that way, where a crossroad is. Get there, be sure to get there just a little 'for twelve o'clock that night so you'll know you'll be there. You have your guitar and be playing a piece sitting there by yourself. You have to go by yourself and be sitting there playing a piece. A big black man will walk up there and take your guitar, and he'll tune it. And then he'll play a piece and hand it back to you. That's the way I learned how to play anything I want.[5]

Though LeDell was insistent on the the supernatural origin of his brother's skills, he notes that Tommy did not give up other music, including religious music. "He used to play anything, don't care what it was. Church song. You could sing any kind of tangled up song you want to, and I'll bet you he would play it."[6]

LeDell was at first enthused about the blues Tommy was teaching him. But he increasingly felt a conflict between his own desire to play blues and his desire for what he considered a righteous life. "I got to the place I decided I'd just give up and quit completely, 'cause I got tired of living a devil's life. I played church songs, but I quit them blues. What made me had to quit them blues, I tried to go over God's word."[7] LeDell's account of his own experience is worth sharing if only to highlight an uncommonly tactile description of a common religious reaction to the blues.

> The last blues that I played was for them old folks. Had that old lady and old man dancing, just dancing and doing the Balling and Jack and doing every kind of funny dance. Old folks, sixty some odd years old, both of them. That was after the war was ceased. That would have been somewhere in '18. That was the last time I played. And I went home that morning 'fore day and hung my guitar up 'side the wall like I been, and every time I dozed off to sleep, the devil would wake me up playing that same piece I had them folks dancing by. And it worried me so, I got up and put the

guitar down on the floor, laid it down on the back, you know, to see what was that playing that guitar. I get back in the bed. By the time I dozed off to sleep, it was playing them blues just like I was playing 'em myself. I got up again and took the guitar and turned it on its strings, laid it down on its string. Went back and dozed off to sleep again and got up. The thing was playing. I got up, and the guitar was turned back up on its back. And whenever I'd get up, it would quit playing. I put it under the bed. I couldn't sleep with it that a' way. I hadn't had that guitar two weeks. I paid seventy-five dollars for it. I got up that morning and told my wife I was through playing a guitar playing blues. I said if I ever play any more, I'm gonna play church songs. I told her I'm gonna sell it. I sold that box for five dollars, just give it away. I didn't want it no more.[8]

The story is an extremely rich account of a personal experience, but it should give us some pause when considering LeDell's story of Tommy's Mephistophelian contract. Are both stories the creations of a very active imagination? The question is relevant since no one has ever corroborated LeDell's story about Tommy's Faustian bargain. As in the case of Robert Johnson, we do not appear to have enough information to judge what was going on in Tommy's inner life. In Tommy's case, we do not even have song lyrics such as we find in Robert Johnson that are suggestive of occult beliefs.

In any case, perhaps more interesting than whether Robert or Tommy Johnson believed they in fact had pacts with dark forces are philosophical or sociological questions about how we might productively interpret the lore of such pacts in the first place. It is worth considering whether in a morally corrupt world, such as the one sanctioned by a system of racial repression in the Jim Crow South, the temptation to embrace what culturally is condemned as dark might be emancipating. In a different context, the embrace of the "anti-Christ" by Nietzsche was understood in a similar vein. If the culture is life- and freedom-denying, as was the case of U.S. culture's embrace of racist politics, then it might seem reasonable to invert the moral logic more fully, to accept that the culturally defined "bad" is actually good and life-affirming. Such an impulse is understandable. But of course, those who embrace the devils in this way would be wise to consider whether their choices are indeed having emancipatory effects on their lives and the lives of others. The embrace of the dark side found in lore of the blues like that surrounding Robert and Tommy Johnson may express a reasonable impulse in an unreasonable world (to channel Theodor Adorno).[a] But very often this rebel instinct, whether in blues, or later in punk or other social movements, succeeds better at deconstructing a false value system than in erecting a valuable one to replace it with.

Returning to our narrative, we can certainly do better to explain Johnson's musical development than turn to occult explanations. We can determine some of the concrete influences on Johnson's musical development by looking to his early musical travels. David Evans underlines that while on his early wanderings, Tommy had already met Will Born and Charlie Patton; and his songs strongly show their influence, as well as that of others who he met while a traveling musician, especially in the Drew area, an area where he would also later spend considerable time.[10]

When returning to Crystal Springs, he worked as a traveling musician in the area for some time. But in 1914 or 1915, still under the age of 20, he married Maggie Bidwell, his first of four wives. He then moved to Jackson with her and later to Drew. This relationship, like his others, was short lived. But it again brought him to the area at the heart of the development of early Delta blues.[11]

In the period under discussion, blues still exhibited strong regional differences. There were not national recordings of country blues musicians. The genre was largely being spread by musicians who played at train stations or as part of minstrel shows. Evans focuses on the particular importance of the music of the Drew region on Johnson's development in this period. Johnson was just one of many musicians to move there, in part to take advantage of the possibility of making money from some of those who migrated from Jackson to pick cotton in that part of the Delta. Drew is in Sunflower County, the same county as Dockery Plantation, the home of numerous blues legends. It is also about 10 miles from the Parchment prison, where various notable blues musicians, such as Son House, served prison sentences.

Patton was the most influential of the early blues players from this part of the Delta. He was born around 1881 and moved with his family to Dockery's plantation in 1897. He had been playing music since he was 14, also with members of the Chatman family. Patton had influenced Henry Sloan, who some speculate was the musician that W.C. Handy, the first to make the blues commercially successful, had seen in Tutweiler, Mississippi, about 15 miles from Drew. This speculation is because Sloan sang a song with the lyrics that Handy had recounted hearing in the story about his first encounter with the blues: "I'm going where the southern cross the dog." The reference is to where the Southern Railway and the Yazoo Delta Railway (the Yellow Dog) meet, in Moorhead, Mississippi.[12] Patton also had taught Willie Brown. Besides having learned from these musicians, Johnson had lived in Drew with Josie Bush, a woman who Evans notes performed blues with the same aptitude as Johnson himself. In addition, Ben Maree, another Drew musician, is said to have strongly influenced Johnson's playing.[13]

Throughout the 1920s Johnson's life was transient. Besides living in Drew, he lived in Jackson, Crystal Springs, and Rolling Fork. He played music in small towns throughout the region. In this time he also influenced many of the musicians of the area. Johnson's music generated some enthusiasm both inside and outside the black communities. He had a white boss, Mr. Campbell, who for some time in the 1920s supported Johnson's musical endeavors. Campbell was a bridge contractor, who gave Johnson a place to stay and also made him a foreman over the bridge work when he was away. But of special importance was Campbell's support for Johnson's music. He would hire him to play music and was supportive of his desire to record.[14] Though the information on his erstwhile boss may seem incidental, it is worth highlighting to show the appeal that blues was having outside of the main community toward which it was eventually marketed. This is suggestive of some broader cross-feeding of the musical cultures.

Johnson finally did commercial recordings from 1927-31. Like most of the best known Delta musicians of this time, he was recorded by H.C. Speir in Jackson. Speir, born in 1895 in Prospect, Mississippi, became an iconic music scout, recording not only Tommy Johnson, but also Charlie Patton, Skip James, John Hurt, and The Mississippi Sheiks, among others. Spier had grown up liking black music and eventually opened a recording studio in his mercantile store in Jackson. There he sold records but also did test recordings of artists, which he sent to major record labels. Spier was known for asking musicians to record at least four original songs. In speaking of his original recording session with Johnson, he indicated that they had to do considerable work together to come up with four unique songs for the debut recording.[15] One explanation is that Johnson often repeated the same traditional lyrics in different songs.

David Evans has explored Johnson's songwriting in great detail in his book titled after the Johnson song, "Big Road Blues." His analysis can help us understand why Spier could have had a problem recognizing differences during

Johnson's first recording session. More importantly, his analysis illuminates key elements of significance for the blues songwriting of Johnson that are more generally applicable to the genre. Evans emphasizes that the genre of blues shares various features with the storytelling practices in oral cultures. Oral cultures have been well described by Walter Ong and Milman Parry, among others.[16] In such cultures, ideas are not copyrighted. They belong to a common cultural stock. Story tellers or bards repeat stories for collective use, to preserve the wisdom and moral sensibilities of a people. The attempt in many oral cultures is to repeat the traditional tales in as close to the original form as possible. In fact, practitioners are often convinced that they are fully duplicating the original stories they learned.

In the case of blues, we see similarities to this, but also some differences. In the blues, both musical forms and lyrics are used in common. Yet, the duplication is not attempting to repeat precisely what one has learned as is typical in oral storytelling cultures. Instead, many basic ideas are taken, mixed, and repeated with variation. For example, we see that many of the lyrics of "Big Road Blues" and of Johnson's broader repertoire, like the musical elements of the song, were old and had been passed on among musicians. Similarly they were freely incorporated by others who heard Johnson. Yet musical and lyrical variations were often added. In fact, the personal experience expressed in the variation is very important for blues, as the bluesman and blues woman cultivated the mystique of singing from personal experience.

Ultimately this resulted in great resemblances among material, but not sameness. As Evans notes, "all ten of Johnson's blues display similarities in their lyrics, melodies, and accompaniments to one or more recorded blues by other artists in the Drew tradition."[17] Yet we see repetition with difference. In part the similarities seen in the work of later Delta musicians indicate Johnson's influence. But his own influential style had already incorporated elements of a broader, pre-existing culture, and it of course reflects a cultural norm that doesn't recognize this "sampling" as theft.

"Big Road Blues" is one of the songs on the accompanying album.[18] It belongs to the traveling blues sub-genre, one of the most important sub-genres of the blues. As numerous scholars have pointed out, though the economic conditions of many African Americans had not dramatically improved after enslavement, and the plantation system in some cases turned people into the equivalent of indentured servants, one of the great differences for postbellum African Americans was the freedom to travel. Men's travel songs often highlighted the desire to escape a love gone wrong, to look for a better economic opportunity, or to simply escape the general toughness of life.

This travel song highlights relational woes. In the midst of emotional difficulties, the protagonist of the song sets off down the "big road." But as he announces, he won't be traveling it alone: "If I don't carry you, I'll carry someone else." The blues artist further expresses the frustration informing his decision to travel down the road—namely, the woman he has been involved with has tried to take advantage of him. As he sings with exasperation in the third verse, "What makes you do me like you do, do do?" This lyric, like the first one, belongs to the common stock of ideas circulating among many blues musicians. Here, the story's protagonist recognizes what is happening and will not allow it. In particular in the fourth verse he expresses his concern about being economically taken advantage of: "Take the poor boy's money now, sure Lord, you won't take mine." Finally, though the song is about a relationship ending with some bitterness, the second verse already announces a note of optimism in the midst of this turmoil. Using one of the most common lines of traditional blues to forecast an improved future, the singer intones, "that sun gonna shine in my backdoor someday, and a wind gonna change and blow my blues away."

Johnson had a story about this composition that Ishmon Bracey told: "He was at a supper once, and his girlfriend wouldn't let him take her home. And he told her, well, he'd get somebody else. He wasn't going down that big road by hisself. When he got him another girl, he made a song of it."[19] But the song is largely composed of traditional lyrics and themes. Whatever Johnson drew on from his own experience, much of this song was spun from lyrics of the common cloth of blues culture.

Various of Johnson's songs had similarities to "Big Road Blues." "Maggie Campbell Blues" is one example.[20] It has the same characteristic bass run at the outset. The melody is virtually identical in many places. Even the lyrics are the same in places. Verse 2 essentially matches the earlier quoted lyric of "Big Road Blues": "Now, the sun gonna shine my back door someday, my back door someday. And the wind gonna change, gonna blow my blues away."

Evans underlines the influence of "Big Road Blues," emphasizing that the song demonstrates in a nearly exemplary way how the blues genre spread. Johnson played with numerous musicians throughout the South in the 1930s and 40s. Some, like Willie Lofton, recorded songs strongly reliant on "Big Road Blues." His "Dark Road Blues" is a folk version of "Big Road Blues." "Dirty Mistreater" had different words and a chorus but great similarities to the song. Amos Easton, who recorded as Bumble Bee Slim, also did recordings inspired by "Big Road Blues": "Sad and Lonesome" and "Rough Road Blues." The melody of "Rough Road Blues" is largely taken from Johnson's song, but Bumble Bee Slim plays bottle neck slide, and the song doesn't have the descending bass line that characterizes the Johnson song. "Sad and Lonesome" follows the melody line of "Big Road Blues" throughout most of the song and imitates the call line of the Johnson song "Don't you hear me talkin'?" It features piano, though, with backup guitar. Kokomo Arnold, who also visited the region, recorded "Stop, Look And Listen," a version of the Mississippi Sheiks' "Stop and Listen Blues" that was deeply indebted to Johnson's song, and she also included a verse of "Big Road Blues."[21]

The similarities between these numerous recordings underscore Johnson's influence on musicians in the area. But they also illuminate the character of early blues writing more generally. People borrowed guitar riffs and lyrics, as these were thought part of a broader cultural heritage, not possessions of anyone in particular. This of course led to conflict with the emergent culture and systems of monetizing music that helped some artists make a living but that served the music company publishers much more than the artists themselves.

The conflict between this traditional style of music making and the emergent copyrighting of music plays out in a particularly fascinating way in Johnson's case. One of the earliest copyright infringement conflicts involves "Big Road Blues." The Mississippi Sheiks, a popular guitar and fiddle band, heavily relied on "Big Road Blues" in their song "Stop, Look and Listen." The recording was similar enough to the song that Johnson's label, Victor Records, sued Okeh Records, which had recorded the Sheiks.

Johnson, who had a severe drinking problem, was apparently drunk at the time of the negotiations. He allowed the Sheiks to use the song in exchange for a small amount of money, but he also left mistakenly convinced that he had signed away his rights to record ever again. In the words of his brother, LeDell, who had the same false impression about the outcome of the negotiations as Tommy: "He drank so much he sold his rights, and he couldn't put out no more records....When Tom was broke, he would sell anything to get a drink of whiskey, or a drink of alcorub or anything that'd bring on a drunk."[22]

The copyright laws in the end served the more famous musicians and the record companies better than they served Johnson, who could have benefited from sound legal representation. Johnson was paid poorly in the negotiations with the Sheiks. Like most of the blues artists of this period, Johnson was also paid poorly for his other work. For the early recordings he received $30 and no royalties (the equivalent of about $550 in 2024). The songs sold well enough that, prior to the negotiations with the Sheiks, Johnson was invited back to record again for Victor Records. In these later sessions he recorded "Big Fat Mama Blues," "Canned Heat Blues," and two songs that Victor didn't release: "Louisiana Blues," and "Lonesome Home Blues." From his second session, "Canned Heat Blues" especially captured an issue of personal significance to Johnson, the dangers of drinking homemade spirits during Prohibition.[23] Given the influence of the song and Johnson's own tragic relationship with alcohol, as well as the all-to-common character of this type of tragedy, it is worth spending some time on the song.

In "Canned Heat" the blues protagonist sings of his dangerous passion for drinking, even if it means ingesting alcorub, the euphemism for rubbing alcohol or the alcohol in Sterno fluid: "Crying, canned heat, canned heat mama, crying, sure, Lord, killing me...Takes alcorub to take these canned heat blues." Johnson goes on to sing of waking with canned heat on his mind, despite his rightful fear that it would "kill me dead"—something of a premonition of Johnson's own fate.

During Prohibition (which lasted until the 1960s in Mississippi given state laws) drinking was a particular risk, as it was often enough difficult to find good, or even safe, liquor. Johnson was like many others who, when not finding good liquor, would make do with bad, and he was known for drinking "canned heat." It was a common drink. Yet it left many crippled or dead. Johnson was among those to suffer its deleterious effects. Tommy's brother, Mager, talks about one of the ways Tommy prepared it.

> That canned heat, you know, it was red. It was in those little old cans. When you open it, take the top off the can. He'd strike him a match and burn it, burn the top of it. And he'd put it in a rag and strain it. It's got juice in it. Squeeze the juice out of it into a glass. And then get him some sugar and put it in there. And then some water. And there he'd go.[24]

Bracey is among those who relates the severity of Johnson's well-known drinking problem:

> Drinking was his weakness. That's what killed him. Tommy would drink anything that he could get to. When he was out of whisky, he would drink anything. That's the reason he put out those Canned Heat Blues. He drank canned heat, shoe polish, alcorub, till they put this business in it. He'd drink anything, denature, beer, wine, whisky, anything he'd get to.[25]

"Canned Heat" is the song that more than any memorializes the harsh drinking issues that haunted Johnson's own life. Musically the song is very similar to "Big Road Blues," without the bass line chorus. Like "Big Road Blues," it is played in drop D tuning. As in many of Johnson's songs, here Tommy sings in falsetto, lending the song a haunting quality. The version of "Canned Heat" from his early recording had a particularly strong effect on later performers, being famously covered by the rock band that named itself after the song. But the recordings from his second session did not sell well. Victor records did not record Johnson again.

Johnson did though get an opportunity to record with Paramount.[26] However, the songs from the Paramount sessions—before Johnson's ill-fated negotiations with the Sheiks—didn't sell well either, and they were his last recordings. The prestige of the earlier recordings did provide Johnson with notoriety, which served him for a time. Between the Victor and Paramount recordings, he was able to leverage his artistic reputation to successfully run a café in Jackson, Mississippi, where he also regularly played. But as his siblings relate the story, he spent any profits on alcohol.[27] So he turned again to a life mostly of a traveling musician, with some intermittent farming. LeDell notes that he would sometimes be away for years and not write the family. Throughout his life, Johnson's bouts with alcohol took a heavy toll on him. He was arrested numerous times for drunkenness and put to work on street work gangs. He also regularly got so drunk that he could no longer play music.[28]

By the 1950s the music popular in the Delta had changed. Trumpet Records recorded Sonny Boy Williamson, from the Delta, as well as Big Joe Williams and Arthur 'Big Boy' Cudrup, whose songs would become especially famous in Elvis Presley's versions. They also recorded Luther Huff and Elmore James. The new music was amplified. The lyric content was more focused and thematic than the earlier country blues. Bracey related how, in the midst of this, Johnson declined: "I tried to get him to change. He cried and said he was going to stop drinking, going to join the church, and going to be a preacher. He said he was going to, but he didn't. And shortly after that I heard he was dead."[29]

He died November 1, 1956, the morning after playing music at a party for his daughter in Crystal Springs. He was buried in Warm Springs Cemetery, north of Crystal Springs, in an unmarked grave.[30] Like many of the blues performers, he lived a conflicted life and died without resolving the conflict.

## Endnotes

[1] Most of what we know of Tommy Johnson comes from David Evans' work. His biography, *Tommy Johnson*, (Studio Vista, 1971) is the only biography on the singer. That book is the source of most of what I provide of Johnson's biography. Evans' writing relies on field work he did in the 1960s. Tommy's brother, Mager, who Evans also recorded, is one of the main sources for Evans' work. Another important source is Evans' *Big Road Blues* (New York: Da Capo Press, 1982). References below are to the biography unless otherwise noted.

[2] Evans, 17.

[3] Evans, 22.

[4] Evans, 22.

[5] Evans, 22.

[6] Evans, 22ff. See Harry M. Hyatt, *Hoodoo – Conjuration – Witchcraft – Rootwork*, vol. 1 (Western Publishing, 1970), 108-111.

[7] Evans, 30.

[8] Evans, 30.

[9] Theodor Adorno, *Minima Moralia: Reflections from Damaged Life*, translated by E. F. N Jephcott (New York: Verso, 2005).

[10] Evans, 23.

[11] Evans, 24.

[12] W. C. Handy, *Father of the Blues: An Autobiography* (New York: Da Capo Press, 1969), 74.

[13] Evans, 25.

[14] Evans, 36ff.

[15] Evans, Big Road Blues, 236.

[16] See, for example, Walter Ong, *Orality and Literacy* (London: Routledge, 3rd edition, 2012). Most of my analysis of oral cultures draws on Ong's work. Cp. Milman Parry, *The Making of Homeric Verse*, edited by Adam Parry (Oxford, Oxford UP, 1971), Albert B. Lord, *The Singer of Tales* (Cambridge, Mass: Harvard UP, 3rd edition, 2020).

[17] Evans, *Big Road Blues*, 236.

[18] Tommy Johnson, "Big Road Blues," Victor Records, 1928, V21279.

[19] Evans, 50.

[20] Tommy Johnson, "Maggie Campbell Blues," Victor Records, 1928, V21409.

[21] Evans, 73.

[22] Evans, 68.

[23] Tommy Johnson, "Canned Heat Blues," Victor Records, 1928, V38535.

[24] Evans, 57.

[25] Evans, 57.

[26] Evans, 61ff.

[27] Evans, 61.

[28] Evans, 82.

[29] Evans, 85.

[30] Evans, 87.

# Chapter 5: Mississippi John Hurt

(Mar. 8, 1893 - Nov. 2, 1966)

In the last years of his life, John Hurt had been the most popular "rediscovery" act of the 1960s blues revival. For a period of about three and a half years, he had been the main folk blues artist attraction at festivals from Newport to Philadelphia and in the college circuit of the U.S. Northeast.

He liked his newfound status. Yet feeling homesick, after about three and a half years in the Northeast, he and his wife returned to Avalon, Mississippi in late 1965 or early 1966.[1] On November 2, 1966, he died of a heart attack in Grenada, Mississippi, a few days after having suffered a stroke while hunting.[2] If accounts can be relied on, he was a blues musician who died happy, as well as well-respected.[3]

Hurt was not one of the bluesmen who reinforced the characterization of the blues as the devil's music. Person after person described Hurt as a kind, gentle man. Stephen Grossman described him as "the grandfather we all wish we had."[4] One of his friends from his Northeast sojourn, Holly Ochs, described him in terms quite strikingly different from those we tend to associate with the bluesmen. While he stayed with Holly and her husband, Max, in New York in the period when he was playing shows in the Northeast, she recounts: "No matter how early we woke on Sunday, John was up earlier, sitting in a chair by the window, dressed in his Sunday best, reading the bible."[5] Though he was not known as a churchgoer and he was a heavy drinker, he was thought to say his prayers every night. He is also recounted as having told his nephew, "Don't ever let anyone tell you there ain't no God."[6]

His mix of blues, folk and gospel touched a nerve during the 1960s blues revival. In this period Hurt was the most sought after of all the earlier blues acts. David Evans, the blues biographer, noted, "Frankly, there just wasn't that much interest in...any of the blues artists really, except Mississippi John Hurt."[7] Dick Waterman, a well-known blues revivalist who had rediscovered various blues musicians and also booked Hurt's shows through the company that he named after Hurt's hometown, Avalon, had also noted that shows with Hurt made money. Those with Skip James did not.[8] Comments of Hurt's daughter about his home performances relate a sentiment apparently shared by many in the college and blues festival circuit in the last years of his life: "Watching Daddy John play his guitar, I had often thought there was something magical about him as his fingers fluttered softly over the strings."[9]

Every artist is a product of a place and time. Mississippi John Hurt, as his show name highlights, was a product of Mississippi—more specifically, Avalon, a small town that had a general store, a post office, and a railway station of the Yazoo and Mississippi Valley Railway. Today the unincorporated town of his birth has but one thing really—the former house of Mississippi John Hurt, which is a museum that features occasional blues shows.

Hurt was born March 8, 1892 (or later according to some public records). He was the last of ten children. In 1901, when he received his first guitar, nothing formally known as "blues" yet existed. Hurt learned his first songs on the guitar from an African American in Avalon, William Henry Carson, who Hurt described as a "finger picker."[10] Besides the direct influence from Carson, about whom little is known, Hurt's early music influences were from the music of minstrel shows and traveling bands, as well as interactions with white musicians near Avalon. He indicated that the first songs he learned were "Hop Joint" and "Good Morning Miss Carrie." He eventually recorded both songs, which were well-known ragtime or "coon" songs (the pejorative name associated with songs that were popular in minstrel shows). These songs feature alternating bass and syncopated rhythms typical of Hurt's work. A lot of the music Hurt learned went back to the 19th Century: "Frankie," "Stack O'Lee Blues," "Funky Butt," "Hot Time in the Old Town Tonight." "Frankie" was based on a famous incident in 1890 in which Frankie Baker killed Allen Bitt, a ragtime pianist in a St. Lous bar. Like "Frankie," "Stack O'Lee" was also based on a well-known barroom incident, from 1895, though the story eventually took on mythical dimensions. Stack O'Lee also involves a murder. Stack kills a man for stealing his Stetson hat and is eventually hanged for this and other crimes. There were versions of these songs by both white and black musicians.[11]

Though many blues biographers highlight that H.C. Speir asked African American artists to record their own blues songs, this served as a rule of thumb not an absolutist policy, as Hurt's recordings with Speir attest. Indeed, according to Newman I. White's study, at least as an industry standard, this may have been a pretty loose rule: over 25 percent of the songs recorded by black artists he sampled had been written by whites.[12] Though his sampling may skew things, the point is that traditional white American music was recorded by some blues artists. Hurt is one of the blues musicians who best epitomizes the intersection of white and black influences that went into what became classified as blues.

While Hurt was known in the blues revival for country blues, few of the country blues artists demonstrate the genre classification problem as clearly as he does. Paul Garon suggests that Hurt, like other artists who played traditional folk songs, are best characterized as "songsters," who only later became blues artists. Indeed, in Garon's view, Hurt did some blues but he mostly remained a songster.[13] He does in any case display the enigmatic character that music genre classification at times has. Throughout his life, Hurt indicated his love of both traditional song and white songwriters. In his earlier life, he played music with numerous white musicians, included Doc Boggs, who was a white musician influenced by the blues.[14] In his earliest days in Avalon he played dances with the white violin player, Willie Narmour, who went on to a recording career and who also recommended Hurt to Okeh Records in 1928. Late in his life he indicated that he greatly admired Jimmie Rodgers, a taste he shared with numerous other blues players.[15]

Hurt's only early recordings before his "rediscovery" were with the Okeh label in 1928. The recordings included many traditional folk songs, including "Frankie" and "Stack O'Lee."

Hurt did lend these songs his personal touch. However, as was the case with Hurt and some others, the music was classified as blues mostly because it was recorded by a black musician for a black music label. In many cases, early blues genre classification had as much to do with marketing as with musical style.

Hurt's music had a small run with the Okeh label, but none of the songs were hits; and he was not asked to record again. The Depression likely played a role. It came on the heels of Hurt's record release. By the early 1930s every major label had declared bankruptcy, with the exception of Victor and Columbia (of which Okeh was a sub-label). The labels that remained in business reduced the number of artists they produced.

As the well-known saying goes, during the Depression, African Americans were the first fired and the last hired. This also applied to the record business. During the Depression black unemployment was two to three times higher than white unemployment. In this context, few people had money for records. Race record sales tanked, decreasing from about five percent of total record sales in 1927 to one percent by 1931.[16] By the time of the blues revival in the 1960s Hurt was living in obscurity. He rarely played music at all, and when he did, his shows were poorly attended. Long after his recording career had appeared to have ended, nobody would have guessed that the obscure musician from Avalon would be the only reason for the town being on the map by the year 2000 or that there would be a museum to honor his contribution to American music.

Instrumental to Hurt's resurgence were especially the efforts in the early 1960s of a few white Northeasterners who became increasingly fascinated by 78s of old country blues players like Hurt. A few records including traditional blues were released in the early 1950s and the 1960s. Harry Smith published an *Anthology of American Folk Music* in 1952, including John Hurt's "Frankie" and "Spike Driver Blues." This facilitated the rediscovery of Hurt by the record collectors of the 1960s like Dick Spottswood, who was instrumental in leading the search for early blues artists.[12] The British skiffle craze also led to some artists recording songs for which Hurt was known: "John Henry" and "Stackolee." As the blues resurgence arrived, Tom Hoskin's was particularly instrumental to Hurt's later career and then to his legacy.

The white largely college educated crowd in the Northeast United States that was behind the national resurgence of interest in the blues often had quite explicit political ambitions. Like John Hammond and like the earlier scholars of the Harlem Renaissance, many of the blues revivalists thought that promoting black artists could help shift the racial dynamic in the United States. Part of the allure of the traditional blues was thus caught up in the 1960s political dynamics. Yet, while that was true of the white blues enthusiasts, quite a few of the blues players, reared in a very racially divisive and dangerous South, were anything but explicitly political. Hurt provides an almost casebook example. He almost never breached the topic of politics.

Hurt's reluctance to talk about politics may reflect that he found keeping peace and getting along with others was best served by a polite demeanor and avoiding controversy. Hurt's biographer, Philip Ratcliffe, in any case spoke aptly of "his strong commitment to avoid offending people."[18] He also didn't care to speak in great philosophical or metaphysical terms about his music—perhaps for similar reasons. For example, in 1966 when he was asked to speak about blues in a workshop at the University of Cincinnati, he simply said: "I will let my music speak for itself tonight." He then proceeded to play a song.

More specifically related to politics, Ratcliffe also recounts that "If any racism arose or if the subject of civil rights came up, John would register some recognition, but would never get involved in any discussion."[19] About the most forceful comment about politics he is recounted as saying occurred in the height of the civil rights movement, when in discussions about Dr. Martin Luther King's movement, Hurt noted: "The chickens are coming home to roost."[20]

These reactions are quite understandable given the socio-political context of the South at the time. Even in 1962, in Mississippi no more than 6.7 percent of African Americans were registered to vote.[21] Mississippi had successfully legislated for segregation even after the Supreme Court case "Brown versus the Department of Education." Expressing the views of many of the white Mississippians, Alabama governor, George Wallace, had, in his inaugural speech, described the "tyranny" of civil rights, suggesting, in a truly contorted logic, that preserving segregation was about preserving freedom. "In the name of the greatest people that have ever trod this earth, I draw the line in the dust and toss the gauntlet before the feet of tyranny, and I say segregation now, segregation tomorrow, segregation forever."[22]

The racism in the deep South was terrifying, quite literally, and had the desired effect of intimidating black Americans to stay out of politics and adopt a deferential stance toward whites. Just six miles from Avalon, where Hurt had spent nearly all of his life, was the setting of the famous case of Emmett Till in 1955. Till's tragic murder occurred in Money, Mississippi, where Hurt's granddaughter had gone to school. There, with friends outside a shop, Till allegedly whistled at the woman store owner. Local white boys became outraged by Till's perceived impertinence, and later abducted him from his nearby uncle's cabin. They beat him, shot him, and threw his body into the Tallahatchie River. An all-white jury later found the white assailants innocent. The case outraged the nation. But it was business as usual in Mississippi. This was the background against which Hurt developed deference as a coping mechanism.

While Hurt did not discuss his views of politics in interviews, he did play many songs, like "John Henry," that became important as part of the folk revival and the civil rights movement. Such songs expressed common travails of the day that were pertinent for black communities. His song, "Pay Day," recorded on the album accompanying this book, offers another example of a story that is political in a broad sense, though without explicitly taking up politics.[23] It underlines economic and relational difficulties that were common in the rural South and that were magnified by political realities.

The song thematizes a particular difficulty in a relationship, exacerbated by poverty, as the male protagonist is waiting for "payday" so that he can relieve himself of the burden of a broken relationship and take his estranged partner back to her mother: "Done all I can do, but can't get along with you. Gonna take you to your mama, Payday." The chorus simply repeats that the protagonist will take his partner to her mother come payday. Apparently, the song's protagonist can't even afford to end a bad relationship with the decency of bringing his partner to her family—at least not until his next check comes in. The song mentions various episodes as the protagonist waits for his payday and then finally takes his partner to her family home. The second verse suggests an economic malaise heightened by another mouth to feed. For many in rural black and white America in the 1920s and 1930s, hunting and fishing supplemented one's pay, allowing people to get food on their tables. If you wanted meat for your meal, you needed to hunt to get it, or you might rely on a hunting dog. Hurt sings of his lack of a dog: A rabbit is at bay, which could make for a satisfying meal, but because he lacks a hunting dog, it gets away. Hurt then again returns to the chorus of waiting for payday to resolve his relational conflict.

The final verse of the song relates the difficulties that ensue even once the protagonist has been paid and is able take his partner home. The situation is still fraught with danger in a time when police harassment based on race was normal and there were still plenty of "sundown towns," municipalities that didn't allow African Americans to enter after dark. Towns with these ordnances existed into the 1960s when federal desegregation laws finally prohibited them. As expressed in Hurt's song: The song's protagonist is on the run with hounds to his back, but he'll make it to his "shanty" before the break of day. Payday doesn't bring its desired full relief, but results in a new kind of danger. The returning of his partner brings new risks for the protagonist, as he faces a dangerous trip home. The song relates a sad irony: The song's protagonist can't afford a hunting dog to help him get a rabbit for his meal, but those who chased black men through country villages had their own special hunting hounds for their purpose.

Hurt, as a kindly blues statesman, went on to inspire generations of white country blues players who found great resonance in traditional folk songs played with Hurt's bluesy touch. He in fact embodied many of the gentlemanly features that the proponents of the Harlem Renaissance like Du Bois and Locke thought would help rehabilitate the racist ideas of the dominant white culture of America. Paradoxically, although Hurt avoided explicit forays into discussions of politics, his music was taken up by a political movement in the 1960s and beyond. In ways subtle, like the breakthroughs of leading cultural figures like Jackie Robinson, Hurt, like other blues artists, also played some role in shifting the political sensibilities of race in America.

# Endnotes

[1] Philip Ratcliffe, *Mississippi John Hurt. His Life, His Times, His Blues* (Jackson: University of Mississippi Press, 2012), 180.

[2] Ratcliffe, 196.

[3] Ratcliffe, 201.

[4] Ratcliffe, 161.

[5] Ratcliffe, 168.

[6] Ratcliffe, 201.

[7] Ratcliffe, 172.

[8] Ratcliffe, 172.

[9] Ratcliffe, 193.

[10] Ratcliffe, 16 ff.

[11] Ratcliffe, 21 ff.

[12] Ratcliffe, 28.

[13] Paul Garon, *Blues and the Poetic Spirit* (San Francisco: City Lights Books, 1996), 22ff.

[14] Ratcliffe, 159.

[15] Ratcliffe, 57.

[16] Ratcliffe, 71.

[17] Ratcliffe, 117.

[18] Ratcliffe, 165.

[19] Ratcliffe, 180.

[20] Ratcliffe, 180.

[21] Ratcliffe, 115.

[22] Qtd. in Ratcliffe, 164.

[23] John Hurt, "Pay Day," Vanguard, 1966.

# Chapter 6: Skip James

(June 9, 1902 - Oct. 3, 1969)

In contrast to Mississippi John Hurt, Skip James felt a severe conflict between his religious views and his blues music and lifestyle. On his deathbed, James promised God that he would give up blues if he were allowed to live. "If it please the Lord to restore my health, I ain't studyin' no more blues whatsoever," he is recounted as saying.[1] He had been fighting testicular cancer since being rediscovered by the folk revivalists five years prior to his death, in 1964. It had now reached its final stages. For his part, James was convinced that he was the victim of a curse by a shunned lover and that he was being punished by God.

At the same time, James thought the timing of his death was beyond his control. He was a biblical pre-determinist, which he explained saying it entailed that "whatever it's in for you to get, you'll get."[2] With a view to the end of his life, he thought that when Jesus wanted to take his life, then Jesus would do that.[3] Yet, his best chance for delaying the beckoning of the Lord wasn't to be found in Western medicine but in "root doctors." James was convinced that his illness had supernatural origins, and that it thus couldn't be rightly diagnosed by the Western doctors, who weren't doing much to improve his health condition in any case. As a result, after he moved to the Northeast when being rediscovered, he sought a root doctor in Washington D.C. who he thought offered the best remedy there might be to his "jinx of death."[4] As James put it, "So far as my health is concerned, I wanna find some good herb doctor, not no medical doctor. I don't want to see no specialists."[5] Neither kind of medicine in the end saved him.

James' practical religious views, like those of many blues artists, mixed Christianity with various African or other folk religious practices that had moved underground as those formerly enslaved were forced to convert to Christianity. Such "hoodoo" practices, like those of the herbalists or root doctors, of course existed in the European and the Native American traditions by another name. These remained very alive in the African American experience, as in pockets of white rural Christianity.

James' distrust in the Western medical establishment is hardly surprising given the unequal treatment of African Americans in the medical system. Even at the time of James' death the shameful Tuskegee syphilis experiments were still going on. In these experiments, black men infected with syphilis were studied as their disease progressed. The scandal is that the study continued for decades after penicillin was available that could have saved the lives of numerous participants. News of this study wasn't brought to public attention until 1972, after James' death. But the conditions against which the experiments were possible were those that contributed to the mistrust in Western medicine of James and others in America's black communities. In addition, cancer at this time was typically a death sentence, as little knowledge existed about how to treat it. These factors help explain the appeal of "old time remedies." For his part, James did not see these practices as merely or essentially African in origin. He speaks of "Indian doctors," revering their practices: "You'd hardly ever hear of an Indian bein' very sick in olden times, cause they'd use old-time remedies."[6] James simply believed there were seers with remedies to some illnesses that had an origin "beyond the comprehension" of Western medical practitioners.

Up to his death, James was a professed man of faith, though one who felt he had spent much of his life backsliding. He had explicitly embraced Christianity after first meeting his father as a 28-year old. His father, who had left when James was a boy, had become a preacher and established a seminary in Dallas. He returned to meet his son just after James' first recordings. At that time he beseeched his son to give up blues and embrace religion. The younger James eventually returned with his father to Dallas to study at his father's seminary for three years. For some time he preached, but only informally. His main job with his father was as a pianist; and though his father requested that he give up "the devil's music" and the accompanying lifestyle, James never did. Indeed, even while studying in seminary, he worked as a pool shark, and for part of the time he was supported by a prostitute. Nonetheless, throughout his life he continued with pious professions of faith.

In line with his faith, James often cultivated the outward appearance of a man of piety. He spoke in interviews of selecting some lyrics—for example, in "Special Rider Blues"—

for pietistic reasons. Though many had used the euphemism of a "rider" for a sexual partner, James said he made his word choice in order to avoid explicitly speaking of sex, thinking that explicit references to sex might have a corrupting influence on the young. Choices like this show how his own image of piety was colored by the inverted moral sensibilities generally accepted by the Methodist religion of his time and place. He would take care to veil a sexual innuendo, but could still sing of violence with little moral concern. As he sings in "22-20 Blues": "Sometimes she gets unruly, And she act like she just don't wanna, But I get my 22-20, I cut that woman half in two."[2]

The protagonist's line that he'll "cut that woman half in two" is found in numerous songs. Robert Johnson repeats the lyric in his "32-20 Blues," stylized on James' song.[8] And while any performer might sing of a violent character to express a dimension of life's experience, James' lyrical celebration of violence in 22-20 blues was not merely part of a stage persona. James fought throughout much of his life and carried a pistol, though not a 22-20 as such a gun didn't exist. He admitted to having killed at least one man. His work in violent milieus, at times as a pimp and bootlegger, surely exacerbated this need for lethal protection. But this violent streak wasn't merely due to such circumstances. Up to the end of his life he also threatened to kill the woman who he thought put a death curse on him.

In general, James conveyed views of religion and the blues that were wide spread among many black Americans in the South. Stephen Calt, the only major biographer of James, describes part of James' back and forth with religion as related to his bouts with alcoholism. As Calt puts it, "On a practical level the church acted as a drying-out clinic for him."[9] But despite James' continual misgivings about blues and his blues lifestyle, he could not convince himself to leave the blues behind, even on the threat that it might not only lead to his death, but that it might also compromise his position in the afterlife. James had eyed the possibility. As he once said, "If I'm going to hell, I won't be the only one there."[10]

The devil did loom large in James' mind. In one of his most famous songs, "Devil Got My Woman," recorded on the accompanying record, he places a traditional love loss song within a metaphysical framework, depicting his deeply fundamentalist leanings.[11] Like many blues songs of the 1920s and 30s, this song mixes unique lyrics with standard ones. The opening lines are from James. He would "rather be the devil than to be that woman's man." Despite the rather clear message of these lines, indicating that James no longer wants to be with the song's female antagonist, the song depicts a mind wrought with conflict. The singer relates having a "ramblin'" uneasy mind in the midst of thoughts of the female antagonist of the song. The song is about a love lost. Yet James doesn't view the winning or losing of his lover in mere human terms, but as part of a metaphysical struggle. In James' description of this song in his autobiographical interviews, he claims the lyrics are based on a true story. Yet he conveys the story against a clearly myth-infused understanding of the world.[12]

In interviews, James relates the biblical literalist beliefs that inform his understanding of the song. Similar to the stories described by the 17ᵗʰ century poet, John Milton, James believed Satan had once been one of God's good angels but had rebelled and was thus condemned along with the other rebel angels. As James relates, "He lives in hell, and that's where he has his part. And that's where Satan is walkin' to and fro' in the earth, in the bowels, persuadin' people."[13] Against this background understanding, James' reading of his partner's betrayal of him is not metaphorical. James doesn't just thematize that he has had a tragic relationship with a woman, but he demonizes her—quite literally. "I came in contace [sic] with a companion, and she was so contentious, unruly, and hard to get along with. I just compared her to the devil—one of his agencies. Since doin' that, I just turned her over to him, and I just give her to know that I would rather be the devil than to be her man, because she was so contentious and I couldn't get along with her in no way."[14]

Yet the lyric depicts James' confusion about the relationship. James appears to want and not want his former partner. The devil, he claims, changed his woman's mind, driving her to betray the song's protagonist. But James doesn't then hope for her exorcism and return. That evidently would be to hope for too much. As he says in his interview, he "just turned her over to him [the devil]." As his lyrics continue, he repeats he would rather be the devil himself than to be that woman's man. The lyrics show a man tied up in logical knots. James here suggests *akrasia*, a torn will deriving from simultaneously wanting and not wanting something. They also suggest a case of sour grapes. Since he can't have what he—in some sense—wants, he convinces himself he doesn't want it anyway. More, he convinces himself that what he wanted is evil.

After his first couple of original verses, in the final verse James does what he and many other blues artists do in their song writing: he adds a verse from the standard blues repertoire that blues musicians copied from each other as they might copy guitar turn arounds. Robert Johnson's later "Come Into My Kitchen" is just one of many songs to employ the verse that James uses here about stealing a woman only to have her stolen back again.[15] But the final lines do nothing but deepen the incoherence of the sensibilities that James is conveying. The man who went away with his woman, as the standard blues verse notes, "got lucky." But since James has already related that he would "rather be the devil" than to be with the female antagonist, we can wonder whether the man who ended up with her was that lucky after all. The story is of a love loss and sour grapes, interpreted against a background understanding that actions take place in a world infused with otherworldly agency. James, like many raised in the country's southern churches, doesn't view the religious imagery as merely metaphorical.

Though James is not generally one of the blues musicians thought to have had a Faustian bargain, Calt speculates that James may have believed he had one. He also speculates that he may have been wanted for a capital crime. As James told

Calt in one of their last conversations, "There's a lot of things I never told you. There's a lot you don't know about me.... I fed you on babe's milk."[16] This left James' major biographer sensing he didn't know much about his subject and speculating about what he might not have known. What we do know about James is that his way of life did not focus on the cultivation of his eternal soul in the manner of the churchmen. He spent a lot of time trying to make a living and without qualms about how he did it.

As for his views of blues music: blues was not a tool for his politics or a tool for his religion. He in part pursued it for money. Yet that clearly was not its only allure for him. He underscores how he found it personally moving. In interviews he recounts that even as a nine-year old he was slipping away from home to hear music, mostly country or jazz. But he relates that this music didn't move him much. "I decided if I would ever wanna take up music, I'd try to play something' just as lonesome as I could, to try to take an effect. And then to ease the mind of anyone that was troubled. Course I hadn't heard of blues then, but I decided I would mostly prefer something like blues."[17] Here we already see James' view that music has a cathartic effect, easing the troubled mind. As he elsewhere relates, "The blues ain't nothin' but a dissatisfied mind: you're worried and not content. And sometimes the blues takes to satisfy you."[18]

Music serves as a kind of therapy in a world where one "can't find no heaven no matter where they go," as James sings in "Hard Time Killing Floor Blues," a song performed on the album accompanying this book. Music provides respite from pain or a way to overcome despair. "I always did prefer blues... in music – I always was a blues man since I was a boy."[19] James contrasts the blues to spiritual and classical music. He speaks of the possibility of a spiritual to "revive" and notes what he sees as a tendency of spirituals or classical music to move one to "rejoice," "dance," or "be sociable." But musically and perhaps in his everyday spirituality (in the broad sense) James wasn't as interested in being revived as in being moved the way that blues moved him. Blues doesn't fundamentally work for revival. "There's a different feelin' in the blues," he explains. "The blues is somethin' that's kind of sad. When the blues hits you, that's sorrowful. It makes you feel like you're sad and misused and mistreated."[20] James underlines the transformative affect of music.

In the end, James gave himself to music that he saw as working like a balm to perhaps allow those who listen to it to feel and work through the same sadness as the artist who wrote and sang it. In his interviews, he speaks of church people (who he calls "sancts") who tried to deny their interest in the blues and who publicly rejected the blues as the devil's music. But he says of playing music for such sancts, "As soon as I hit a blues, well that's gonna take more effect. Why? Because it has reached more deeply into the minds of the people. You say for instance this: if you and your companion has had a little disaster, or somethin' arose between y'all, your mind is a little wavery in thinkin' over how she have treated you. You may think about the affection that you have towards her and have shown, and it hurt you a little bit. Then, I could play a jazz and it wouldn't take no effect. I would play a classical piece; it wouldn't even 'tract your attention. I could play a spiritual and you wouldn't listen to it. But I could just hit a blues tone, and that would take such effect until you would feel different."[21]

Blues had the power to make him "feel different." The blues moved him in fact to become a singular guitarist, pianist and musician. His music is marked by a pensive, eerie character. James is known as the stylizer of the Bentonia sound—dark, chilling, and thoughtful—made so in James' case in part by the D-minor tuning of his guitar in many songs, but also by the bleak lyrics. Non-standard tunings were common in blues. It is one of the major characteristics of James' sound. But his lyrics are also non-characteristic of the genre. Hearing James we can indeed wonder how close he came to creating the sound that Handy, the early blues band leader and composer, described as setting him on his career to be the self-professed "father of the blues." Handy described the earliest blues he heard as weird and haunting.[22] The early music chronicler, Charles Peabody, also described his experience of black rural music at the beginning of the 20th century similarly, saying of his first encounter with blues or the precursor to blues, "I have not heard that kind again nor of it."[23] James' sound, with its alternate tunings and his distinctive tenor voice, left many with a similar uncanny feeling. His subject matter deals with many of the common themes of blues, but there is also something poetic and distinctive in his music that is missing from much of the blues. As *Times* critic Robert Shelton described him in 1966: "James is almost the elusive poet of the blues"[24] This is evident in much of his music. "Hard Time Killin' Floor Blues," in particular, though is one of the iconic blues songs of Depression era America that contributed to this assessment of James.[25]

This song, released with Paramount Records in 1931, paints a bleak picture of the times. James, who had known many hard times, depicts times that are yet "harder than [they] ever were before." Since the end of the period of black American enslavement unemployment rates among African Americans had always been high and work conditions harsh. In the early 1900s to the Depression the work conditions of many African Americans were wretched. Yet, the Depression made things even worse. James' haunting music captures the seriousness of the situation, already apparent in 1931. The song's second verse highlights the homelessness that accompanied the unemployment. James sings of people "driftin'," underlining that regardless of where people turn, they "can't find no heaven." The blues spirit is not one that tends to raise the expectation of heaven, to anticipate a place or state beyond conflict, where sadness and suffering are eternally laid aside. This expression of a longing for a final resolution to life's troubles was the domain of spirituals. In America's South of the 1930s about which James sings, certainly black people are not going to find a heaven, and blues is not pointing to one.

Like the protagonist of the song, the individuals for whom James sings are stuck on "the killing floor." The "killing floor" reference is of course metaphorical, with a clear enough meaning, but it had traditionally referred to Chicago slaughterhouses where African Americans were given only the most demeaning of jobs. In this song, though, it is not the cattle that are being slaughtered. As the last line of the song suggests: "these hard times gon' kill you, just drag on slow." The lament in James' version suggests hellish conditions— the antipode to heavenly hopes. Yet James' lyrics do allow a slight glimmer of hope for a change. Still, James doesn't sing optimistically of what *will* happen when he gets off the hard killin' floor, but only *if* he does. And even if he escapes those killin' floor blues, James only dares to hope to "never get down this low no more." There is no expectation not to sink down, certainly none to "rise up" to heavenly glory as one might find in a spiritual. But there is a hope not to fall so low again, so low that death is beckoning on the killing floor.

The song captures something general about James' songwriting. The lyrics and music are pensive, haunting. The original recording of this song, like "Devil Got My Woman," was released by Paramount in 1931. But given that few people had money for records during the Depression, James suffered the plight of most musicians of the time: his records sold poorly. So he achieved neither the notoriety nor the money that he had expected. In fact, Paramount, which had earlier sold between 10,000 and 100,000 of a race record, rarely sold 500 after the onset of the Depression.[26] The label went bankrupt soon after these recordings. James essentially took about a 30-year hiatus from professional blues music after this, until he was rediscovered as part of the folk and blues revival of the 1960s. Peter Guralnick relates James' answer to the question of why he quit performing: "I was so disappointed. Wouldn't you be disappointed man? I cut twenty-six sides for Paramount in Grafton, Wisconsin. I didn't get paid but $40. That's not doing very good. Wouldn't you be disappointed?"[27]

James returned to blues in part because of hopes for some economic benefits. But as his deathbed statements and many documented conversations from this period indicate, he continued to feel uneasy about the blues and the blues life. The rediscovery unfortunately didn't bring the economic boon he had hoped for. Though he played the Newport Folk festival within a few weeks of being rediscovered, the economic payoffs of the revival were insubstantial. He became a significant and somewhat unique voice in the 1960s blues revival, but Guralnick relates that he still was mostly playing crowds of 20-30 people, sometimes fewer. In fact, he could not make a living wage as a musician, even in this period. Still, it was in this revival period that James made his greatest mark on American culture.

James' fundamentalism kept him from giving himself entirely to the blues, but he couldn't pull himself away from the blues either. He had a pragmatic recognition that blues could reach people in a unique way, to allow them to work through pain that is simply an inescapable part of life. Though he intellectually never was able to affirm this as something that was basic to his own mental or spiritual liberation, he also wasn't able to leave it alone.

The philosopher Friedrich Nietzsche is well-known for having criticized Christianity for being life-denying and for arguing that if you really affirm life, it is necessary to affirm its pain and pleasure, not to lose yourself in an illusion of a hereafter where all conflict ends and pain disappears. Nietzsche also argued that music provides the greatest possibility for us to work through such existential pain. It allows us to transform suffering and conflict into beauty.[28] James was able, like Nietzsche, to see this value in music—especially in the blues. He saw it as allowing us to face and process pain. Indeed, James suggests he sees a this-worldly spiritual dimension to the blues, but this conflicted with his dominant fundamentalist vision. In the end, despite the expressive power of the music to which James devoted so much of his life, he was not able to separate blues music from a "blues lifestyle," and he always saw an embrace of the blues as backsliding. Yet, despite his life-long theoretical expressions of a fundamentalist faith, in the end, the religious promise of a heaven where no more conflict existed was not enough to meet the real needs of James' suffering the way that blues and self-medication did. James died a bluesman, conflicted about his love for a spiritually moving music that he in some ways found salvific, but that he was not able to resolve with his Christian pietism and vision of a future life where all pain was resolved and all conflict stilled.

## Endnotes

[1] Stephen Calt, I'd Rather Be the Devil. Skip James and the Blues (Chicago: Chicago Review Press, 2008), 245.

[2] Calt, 178.

[3] Calt, 16.

[4] Calt, 16.

[5] Nehemiah "Skip" James, Blues & the Soul of Man (Stefan Grossman's Guitar Workshop, Inc., 2019), 39

[6] James, 39.

[7] Nehemiah "Skip" James, "22-20 Blues," Paramount Records, 1931.

[8] Robert Johnson, "32-20 Blues," Vocalion, 1927.

[9] Calt, 183.

[10] Calt, 347.

[11] Nehemiah "Skip" James, "Devil Got My Woman," Paramount, 1931.

[12] See James, 23 ff.

[13] James, 23.

[14] James, 23.

[15] Robert Johnson, "Come On In My Kitchen," Vocalion, July, 1937.

[16] Calt, 355.

[17] James, 29.

[18] James, 29.

[19] James, 29.

[20] James, 29.

[21] James, 30.

[22] Handy, p. 77.

[23] Ted Gioia, Delta Blues. The Life and Times of the Mississippi Masters Who Revolutionized American Music (New York: Norton), 2008, 228.

[24] Calt, 293.

[25] Nehemiah "Skip" James, "Hard Time Killing Floor Blues," Paramount, 1931.

[26] Calt, 136.

[27] Peter Guralnick, Looking to Get Lost. Adventures in Music & Writing (New York: Little Brown and Company, 2020), 20.

[28] Friedrich Nietzsche, *The Birth of Tragedy*, edited by Michael Tanner, translated by Shaun Whiteside (London: Penguin Books, 1993).

# Chapter 7: Robert Petway

(c. 1903, death unknown, after 1941)

Not much is known of Robert Petway. It is thought that he was born near Yazoo City, Mississippi, around 1907. The blues biographer and music theorist, Ted Gioia, notes that a social security death certificate lists the birthday of a Robert Petway on October 18, 1907, with a death in Chicago in 1978. But the birthdate doesn't match with the 1920 Leflore County Census, the census for the area where Petway lived at that time. As is the case with so many blues artists, parts of Petway's life are phantomlike.

As a young man, Petway played music around the Greenwood, Mississippi area, often working together with Tommy McClennan. As David Edwards described their relationship: "[McClennan] and Robert Petway had the same style cause they played together all the time...It'd be in and out; sometimes Tommy would be by himself and then when he'd get something pretty large he'd go get Robert."[1] Like McClennan, Petway played a steel-bodied guitar and sang with a heavy voice.

Honneyboy Edwards indicated that Petway had two or three marriages before moving to Chicago. He is said to have had a liking for religious women and to have played in churches at times. But like numerous blues artists, he had conflicting emotions about blues and religion. He went through periods of religious fervor but then backslid. Gioia notes that his conversions from this early period didn't last long. He returned to "performing the blues, drinking whiskey and playing cards."[2]

In the early 1940s Petway went to Chicago, like McClennan. He there recorded 16 blues songs with Bluebird Records, published in 1941 and 1942. These became his legacy. The most famous of these recordings was "Catfish Blues," a song of enigmatic origins that would go on to become extremely influential. The song existed before Petway recorded it. Tommy McClennan and Skip James were known to have played versions. In fact, McClennan recorded a version at about the same time as Petway, entitled "Deep Blue Sea Blues." This had some lyrical differences from Petway's song. As the first to record the song, Petway was typically credited as the composer. His recording enjoyed modest success before being eclipsed by Muddy Waters' later version of the song. Waters retitled the song as "Rolling Stone."[3]

Though little is known of the traditional song, prior to Petway, elements of "Catfish Blues" were known from a 1928 recording of "Jim Jackson's Kansas City Blues" with Vocalion.[4] The first line of the the song is found in Jackson's song. "I wished I was a catfish, swimming down in the sea; I'd have some good woman, fishing after me." Parts 1 and 2 of Jackson's song ostensibly sold a million copies, making it one of the first gold records ever made. However, the line about catfish is included in part 3, which had much less success. Various versions of "Kansas City Blues" that omitted the line about the catfish followed Jackson's. But the line about the catfish was included in the influential 1928 recording by William Harris. For his part, Jackson had played in the medicine show circuit, where the song may have been heard with this lyric as early as 1919.[5] Musically, Jackson's song differs from Petway's, but has a similar repetitive droning guitar.

Petway's recording of the song is characterized by a rhythmically heavy drone, beating out a repeating alternating bass line. The vocals on Muddy Waters's "Rolling Stone" and Jimi Hendrix's "Voodoo Chile" Waters' have a family resemblance to the vocal line of Petway's version of the song, but the guitar parts of each of them are considerably developed from what is found on Petway's early recording.

Petway's song brings together standard lyrics that don't form a coherent narrative. In the first verse, a man is to lay down for rest, but decides to stroll out West, a line well-known from many blues songs including Skip James' "Devil Got My Woman." In the second verse, the protagonist wishes himself to be a catfish that the women would try to hook. The sexual innuendo is clear enough. He imagines what it would be like to be the one being fished for. The third verse offers something of a non-sequitur. It relates the protagonist going to a church where he falls upon his knees but finds he has no words to offer as a prayer. In the final verse the protagonist is basking in the pleasant thought of writing to his "baby," who is thinking of the "little ol' thing called me." Here the protagonist is the one doing the fishing, but the trip is successful. Muddy Waters' version drops the first verse of the Petway song and adds numerous different verses after a verse that approximates the second verse of Petway's version. In Waters' version, the blues protagonist relates the story of his mother telling his father "I got a boy child comin', he's gonna be a rolling stone." The innocence of Petway's recording is also lost as Waters incorporates a line from Tommy McClennan's 1941 version of the song. The man at his lover's steps is asked into the house for an apparent liaison after the woman's husband has gone away. In McLennan's original words: "Walk on in now, my husband just now left."[6]

Over two hundred versions of the song have been reported.[7] Waters' version was his first recording for Chess Records and sold around 70,000 copies. It featured him alone on an electric guitar. He reworked the song in 1951 into "Still a Fool." This recording included a bass drum, played by Leonard Chess, and a second guitar, played by Little Walter, as well as variations in the lyrics.[8] In many live recordings Waters intermixed the lyrics of the two songs. Various versions of the song were also recorded around the time of Waters' release. Bob Thomas did a version in 1951 with Sonny Boy Williamson II on harmonica. It was recorded with Lillian McClennan, the wife of Petway's early musical partner. That song was originally released with Trumpet. Lillian later also recorded a variation with Elmore James. James apparently didn't want to record the song but McClennan recorded it with Sonny Boy Williamson II on blues harp as they practiced in the studio. It was released as the B side to Elmore James' single of "Dust My Broom," which made the R&B top ten charts in 1952.[9]

Larry Johnson recorded a version of the song released either in 1962 or 1967 that has greater similarities both musically and lyrically to Muddy Water's later influential version. Mager Johnson, Tommy Johnson's brother, who both Ishmon Bracey and Roosevelt Holts reportedly thought was a better guitar player than his brother, released recordings of the song in 1966 and 1969."[10] It, like most versions after Muddy Waters' recording, also has greater similarities to Muddy Waters' rendition. Muddy Waters' version also lyrically inspires Jimi Hendrix's take on a song in "Voodoo Chile." Muddy Waters version and new title ("Rolling Stone") were also the inspiration for the name of the British rock band who, while looking for their band name are said to have eyed the song name from a Muddy Waters' album and then to have taken their band name from that. The newly named song became more associated with that band than with anything that had come before.

## Endnotes

[1] Paul Oliver, *The Story of the Blues* (Boston: Northeastern U P, 1997), 141ff.

[2] Ted Gioia, *Delta Blues* (New York: Norton & Company, 2009), 212.

[3] "The Obscure Origins of a Blues Classic, Catfish," www.knkx.org/jazz-and-blues/2013-07-19/obscure-origins-of-a-blues-classic-catfish-blues, accessed April 24, 2024.

[4] Jim Jackson, "Jim Jackson's Kansas City Blues, Part 3," Vocalion, 1928.

[5] McKinley Morgenfield, "Rolling Stone," Chess Records, 1950.

[6] Robert Petway, "Catfish Blues," Bluebird Records, 1941. Petway's version is not precisely duplicated on the accompanying album. There I also make up one verse. Cp. Muddy Waters "Rolling Stone" (noted above) and Tommy McLennan, "Deep Blue Sea Blues," Bluebird Records, 1941.

[7] Herzhaft, Gerard (1992). "Catfish Blues." *Encyclopedia of the Blues*. Fayetteville, Arkansas: University of Arkansas Press, p. 442, https://archive.org/details/encyclopediaofblooherzh/page/442, accessed June 21, 2024.

[8] Robert Gordon, *Can't Be Satisfied. The Life and Times of Muddy Waters* (New York: Little Brown and Company, 2002).

[9] Robert Palmer, *Deep Blues* (New York: Viking Press, 1981), 214. For further comments, see Max Haymes, "Catfish Blues (Origins of a Blues)," https://earlyblues.com/essay_catfish.htm, accessed July 16, 2023.

[10] David Evans, *Big Road Blues*, 220.

# Chapter 8: Lightnin' Hopkins

## (Mar. 15, 1912 - Jan. 30, 1982)

Lightnin' Hopkins waxed more philosophically about the blues than nearly any of the other blues artists. He often describes blues as an existential condition.

> When you born into this world, you born with the blues. Worry is the blues. Upset is the blues.... Trouble is the blues. You can have the blues about being broke, about your girl being gone. You can have the blues so many different ways till it's hard to explain. But whenever you get a sad feeling, you can tell the whole rotten world you got nothing but the blues[1]

In his 1964 folkway interviews with Sam Charters, released as *My Life in the Blues*, Hopkins underlines that the blues is a feeling of sadness that may be brought on by specific conditions and may be alleviated or disappear: "The blues is a feeling....You can be happy. People say you don't have no blues when you're happy.... But just like you say, you lose something, or your wife quits you or your girlfriend quits you, or maybe you wants a suit of clothes and you don't have no money to buy 'em with..., that's the blues, man.... A worry is the blues. And when you get worried you just go to tell the world, say, 'I got the blues'."[2]

In his statements on the blues, taken as a whole, we see he sometimes treats blues as existential, sometimes as born of personal circumstance, and sometimes as a musical form.

In the quotes from his interviews, he also suggests a need to enunciate the fact that you have the blues. As the quotes above illustrate: "You just go tell the world, say, 'I got the blues'"; or "you can tell the whole rotten world you got nothing but the blues." Hopkins suggests the power of blues music and the power of the enunciation that one has the blues to expunge the blues (understood as a feeling of sorrow). Playing the blues and speaking about blues makes it possible to overcome the blues. Yet it seems fair to surmise from Hopkins' comment that we are to enunciate our blues to a "rotten world" that we will not permanently leave the blues behind. Hopkins appears rather Nietzschean in his assessment that at an existential level some suffering and sadness will remain or recur.

In the folkways interviews Hopkins relates some of the details of his personal background that created the context for his own blues. Among those contributing factors, he relates that his father had killed a man and served time in the penitentiary. Soon after he got out, when Sam was just three years old, his father was killed. Sam was then raised under difficult economic circumstances, and in a context accompanied by violence. One of his brothers was also killed— as a 17 year old. These are the situations that contributed to his blues; and he turned to music very early in life, perhaps as a cathartic way of dealing with such difficulties —assuming his early motivations for making music are similar to his later ones. As he said, "I been making up songs all my life, ever since I was eight years old when I got out on my own"[3]

For the young Hopkins making music may have allowed him to work through some personal difficulties. It also allowed him to avoid field work that many around him toiled in. However, it did not keep him from trouble. Early in his life he was often in trouble with the law. As he noted in early interviews, "I've been on a chain gang four times."[4] One incident was for a fight where he encouraged his cousin to "cut" a guy they were fighting, which his cousin did. He continued to get in trouble and, at least early on, was relatively hardened to the punishments. He relates, "Jail didn't mean nothing to me then. You could put me in there every day."[5] Hopkins had lived a hard and eventful life from an early age. He grew up fast as his line about getting "out on his own" at the age of eight clearly indicates. While still a teenager he had done farm work, traveled through areas of Texas, worked as a street musician, and been put in jail. He married at age 16. Throughout this time, he had a violent temper and often became embroiled in fights. It is rumored that he stabbed Ida Mae Gardener, with whom he had been in a relationship.[6] But he eventually succeeded in largely avoiding these kinds of troubles. The music opened up another world for him.

In the folkways interviews Hopkins relates stories of his life as a child where he first heard blues music and learned to play it. One of his earliest exposures to blues music was through Albert Hawley, a blues player who dated his mother when Sam was seven. Hopkins tells of Hawley sitting on the edge of the bed, playing guitar. Individual guitar players like Hawley were his original inspiration.

But in the folkways interview he notes two other experiences that were especially formative. One was after he had a guitar for a while and saw Blind Lemon Jefferson, the first Texas country blues artist to have great national success with blues recordings. The often told story is that young Sam was playing some notes on a guitar when Blind Lemon heard him. Though Blind Lemon was at first irritated, when he heard this young boy picking out the notes like he did, he was sympathetic. The crowd then turned its attention to and celebrated the young boy. The other key experience was when he was 20 and met Texas Alexander, who he claimed was his cousin. Texas Alexander, though not as renowned as Blind Lemon, was another of the first nationally known county blues recording artists. As Hopkins explains, Alexander carried a guitar for others to play as he accompanied them as a singer. What especially impressed Hopkins as a young man was not just the life of music making but that Texas Alexander could afford a Cadillac. Against the backdrop of the economic difficulties Hopkins had experienced, this economic success was an inspiration. Joining the road with Texas Alexander provided Hopkins with one of his earliest musical opportunities. He only stopped working as Texas Alexander's accompanist in the late 1930s.[2]

Hopkins was born in 1912 in Centerville, Texas. In counter-distinction to most country blues artists on the accompanying album, he first became nationally renowned as one of the early generation of electric blues guitar players. Through the 1940s and 50s he did numerous recordings with electric guitar. Indeed, his extensive discography, listed in Alan Govenar's *Lightnin' Hopkins, His Life and Blues,* shows that from his first recordings in 1946 to 1954, only 3 recordings of his 31 recording sessions were with acoustic guitar.

However, when "rediscovered" during the folk revival by Charters and McCormick, he was pushed into playing more acoustic guitar. When Charters met Hopkins, Hopkins had pawned all of his instruments. So Charters had to buy him one; and despite Hopkins' own preference for an electric guitar, Charters bought him an acoustic.[8] This set the stage for a different trajectory in his development, as he went on to make many great acoustic blues records in addition to the early electric ones. The choice for an acoustic guitar was because Charters was planning to unleash Hopkins on a folk scene, with numerous purists who did not want to hear electric guitar. Even years after Hopkins' rediscovery some members of that folk scene would agonize over Bob Dylan playing electric guitar at the Newport Folk festival. In fact, at the famous 1965 festival when Dylan went electric, Hopkins' played acoustic guitar. The hostilities between folk purists and the fans of electric guitar during this festival were so explosive that Dylan's manager, Albert Grossman, got into a fistfight with Alan Lomax over Dylan's decision to opt for the electric sound. Hopkins by this time had long accommodated to the wishes of genre purists when playing such venues, despite what appear to have been his oft countervailing music instincts. Over the long run, Hopkins' own ability to bridge the acoustic and electric musical worlds, which to some extent overlapped with the more urban and the more country ones, turned into a part of his broad appeal.

As noted, long before Hopkins went electric, he had played acoustic guitar with Texas Alexander in the early 1920s. At this time, guitarists were still strongly influenced by regional musical styles since there were not yet many national recordings to draw on. Yet, however much Hopkins was influenced by musicians in the early Texas tradition, his own first recordings, in 1946, came about 20 years after the releases of Blind Lemon Jefferson and Texas Alexander with Lonnie Johnson. At this time, there may were lingering regional differences in musical styles, but Hopkins had come under many national influences as well. He blended these into a unique musical mix. Over the span of his recording career, he became a force of his own, with considerable influence. As Jimmy Vaughn puts it: "I don't think there could be a B.B. King, or a Buddy Guy, or Jimmy Hendrix, or a Stevie Ray Vaughn without Lightnin' Hopkins." B.B. King has a similar estimation, stating that without Lightnin' Hopkins, "the blues would never have been like what it turned out to be.... He was a great player. He didn't put sugar on anything. He just played it"[9]

One of the most impressive things about Hopkins' is the sheer volume of his output. Govenar's discography covers over 45 pages. Such productivity was in part because Hopkins freely disregarded record company contracts. As Govenar notes, at various points in his life "he'd record for anyone who gave him a hundred dollars a song."[10] He recorded numerous blues standards, often with his stamp both musically and lyrically. He also often composed blues lyrics on the spot, in many cases using some traditional lines as anchors, as was common in the tradition.

Hopkins' music dealt with a broad spectrum of themes. In "Shinin' Moon," a song on the accompanying record, he sings of an affair.[iii] He recorded many versions of the song, with lyrics varying somewhat in the different versions. Different renditions of the first two verses were minor. But a final verse was sometimes completely changed. The first of these recordings was in 1947 with Gold Star. In the opening lines the protagonist is waiting under the moon light, looking up at his lover's window. In the second verse, the protagonist secretly gazes at his lover. Hopkins sings of the character who tiptoes to the window to watch his lover sleep. His excitement is palpable, as the sight of her is enough that he wants to "jump...through the keyhole in her door," a clear enough sexual innuendo. In the third verse the protagonist wishes his lover to come to the window so he can "whisper" words that, as he sings, "I don't want your man to hear." The suggestion of an affair here is already pretty clear, but in Hopkins' 1960 recording the suggestion is clearer still. As Hopkins sings in this version, "Every night about the break of day, you know the home is happy when your baby gone away." Here we see an inversion of traditional values. The happy home not the one where a married couple celebrate their union but where the husband or regular partner is "gone away" and the illicit lovers' rendezvous can commence. The song effectively draws on images of the shinin' moon, the night, the breaking dawn, in describing the run up to the act of marital infidelity.

Hopkins' "Jail House Blues" of 1949 was a rendition of a Bessie Smith song, but to which Hopkins added his own final verse and dropped two of hers.[12] Hopkins' addition articulates a sensibility that differed from that of his younger self, who said jail didn't mean a thing to him: "Hey, mister jailer," Hopkins intones, "Will you please sir bring me the key, I just want to open the door, 'Cause this ain't no place for me." Hopkins repeats that final line in his song "I Worked Down on the Chain Gang."[13]

In contrast to "Shinin' Moon," in "Jail House Blues" and numerous other songs, Hopkins sang of topics that can be viewed as political in the broad sense, though the whiskey drinking man who also toted a gun was not anybody's image of a protest singer. In any case, many of his songs articulate difficulties common to black Americans of the mid-twentieth century. His rendition of "Backwater Blues," which like "Jail House Blues" was by Bessie Smith, is one of many other recordings that describes troubles that were especially acute for African Americans. Hopkins titled the song "That Mean Old Twister."[14] In this song, as in many of his renditions of earlier blues recordings, Hopkins' arranges the song for guitar and changes some of the lyrics. Among other things, in his recording, he describes not only a flood, but also a "twister." Tornados were another natural phenomenon, like floods, that wreaked havoc on all indiscriminately. Yet they caused especially harsh affliction to the marginalized and generally poor African American communities, given their already precarious economic situation.

Dr. Cecil Harold, a manager of Hopkins in his later career, noted that "Lightnin' could put into words the mood of the black community."[15] He emphasized that this was in particular true of "a black community that was hit especially hard by the Great Depression."[16] Hopkins' first song to make the national charts certainly demonstrates this skill. On February 12, 1949 "Tim Moore's Farm" reached number 13 on the Billboard charts of most played juke box songs for race records. It was a traditional song, protesting a gratuitously cruel plantation owner in Grimes County, Texas. The song narrator laments having moved to Tim Moore's farm, as "the one thing...this black man has done wrong." Tim Moore's inhumanity to his worker is extreme. In the course of the story the protagonist receives a telegram that his wife has died, but Mr. Moore is dismissive. Rather than humanely allowing the sharecropper to take time to mourn and to deal with the affairs of his wife's passing, he tells the song protagonist that he had better finish his field work. Throughout the song, Mr. Moore disregards the husband's affliction. Only late in the song is it suggested that the protagonist may bury his wife, but only during one of his "dinner times." The sharecropper's emotional state and need to deal with the affairs of his wife and family are not Mr. Moore's concern, and the burial won't happen on Mr. Moore's time.[17]

The lyrics were unfortunately all too easy for sharecroppers—and other exploited laborers—to identify with, even in the late 1940s. Few of Hopkins' other early blues hits are as overtly political. "T Model Blues," which was #8 on the R&B jukebox charts on October 8, 1949, is a song full of double entendre in a similar vein to Robert Johnson's "Phonograph Blues." While the sexual undercurrents of the song are standard in blues, the self-irony of Hopkins' song here about male impotence puts the song in a different class than the more macho "Hoochie Coochie Man" or "Mannish Boy" that become popular electric guitar hits for Muddy Waters within a few years, or various other songs that become hits for Hopkins.[18] Many of Hopkins' stream of hits following these early successes are thematically more standard blues fare such as "Shotgun Blues" and "Little School Girl."

In contrast to Johnny Lee Hooker and Muddy Waters, Hopkins managed to continue his musical career success for some time without touring. But by the mid-1950s, Hopkins had reached the high point of his early electric blues career. Rock'n'roll had begun to emerge as a more commercially successful music genre. He did no recordings between 1955 and 1959.

Only with the emergence of the folk revival did Hopkins regain some of his earlier success. Sam Charters book, *The Country Blues*, published in 1959, was instrumental to Hopkins' re-emergence, as was the already discussed work of McCormick. Charters book opens with a depiction of Hopkins as a rough raw singer of a bygone era. As he writes of Hopkins in the final chapter of the book: "Lightnin', in his way, is a magnificent figure. He is one of the last of his kind, a lonely, bitter man who brings to the blues the intensity and pain of the hours in the hot sun, scraping at the earth, singing to make the hours pass."[19] This re-introduction of Hopkins has similarities to John Lomax's earlier re-introduction of Leadbelly in the late 1940s. Though both men had years of musical careers behind them in urban settings, they were marketed as country blues players. Despite Hopkins' already substantive R&B success and his over 30 recordings with electric guitar targeted mostly at an urban black audience, Hopkins is described as "a genuine folk artist" and "pure country."[20] Hopkins did easily blend musical worlds.

More easily than many blues artists, Hopkins also blended other worlds that were often culturally divided. Hopkins' precise religious views are not entirely clear. But in contrast to many of the blues performers, he was not haunted by internal conflict between religious ideas and his music and lifestyle. He at times spoke of the blues as a kind of spiritual disposition. When asked what made him different from others, he said, "A bluesman is just different from any other man that walks this earth. The blues is something that is hard to get acquainted with. Just like death. The blues dwell with you everyday and everywhere."[21] He saw blues as a type of disposition and an accompanying lifestyle, but without a negatively judgmental eye deprecative of its value.

Hopkins lived his life, dwelling with the blues like few others. But on January 30, 1982, he died of cancer of the esophagus at St. Joseph's Hospital in Houston, Texas. The man who carried a loaded shotgun in the back seat of his car, preferred Gordon's gin, and played blues like no one before him was buried at Johnson's Funeral Home Chapel at 2301 McGowen Street in the Third Ward of Houston, the area where he had spent most of his adult life. About 1,000 mourners attended his funeral. The service had organ music; and Rocky Hill, a Houston musician who at times played with Hopkins, also played a standard bottleneck blues song and "Amazing Grace." The blues at the funeral is said to have bothered some of the attendees. That this sentiment existed into the 1980s— and would be expressed at the funeral of a blues master— indicates how strong the puritanical movement remained within the community that birthed the blues.[22] Hopkins did not share the sentiment.

Hopkins' occasional singing of religious songs was one element leading his daughter to surmise that he was a religious believer. He did in any case record some good religious blues songs. "Got Nowhere to Lay My Head," is one of Hopkins' most expressive songs of the genre. He introduces the song speaking of being on his "bending knees." As the song continues, he shows compunction for some things in his life, but not the kind that suggests a need to give up the blues. He says, "I asked the good Lord to forgive me, oh Lightnin' won't do them things no more."[23] Then in this recording as in so much of his life, he leaned into his guitar and prayed a bluesman's prayer.

## Endnotes

[1] Les Blanks, director, *The Blues According to Lightnin' Hopkins* (Les Blanks Films, 1970), qtd. in Alan Govenar, *Lightnin' Hopkins. His Life and Blues* (Chicago: Chicago Review Press, 2010), 12.

[2] Hopkins, *My Life in the Blues,* Prestige Records , LP 7370, 1964.

[3] The Blues According to Lightnin' Hopkins, also qtd. in Govenar, 12.

[4] The Blues According to Lightnin' Hopkins, also qtd. in Govenar, 13.

[5] The Blues According to Lightnin' Hopkins, also qtd. in Govenar, 13.

[6] Govenar, 15-18.

[7] Govenar, 30.

[8] Govenar, 74.

[9] The Greatness of Lightning Hopkins, compiled by Andria Rogavia, accessed 5/27/2024.

[10] Govenar, 135.

[11] Sam Hopkins, "Shinin' Moon," Gold Star 613/Modern 20-543, 1947. The version of this song on the album doesn't precisely duplicate Hopkins lyrics. Compare the 1960 recording with Bluesville, LP 1019.

[12] Sam Hopkins, "Jail House Blues," Gold Star 662/Sittin' In With 644, 1949.

[13] Govenar, 14.

[14] Lightnin' Hopkins recorded a version of Smith's song, retitled "That Mean Old Twister," 1946, Aladdin 167. Hopkins arranged the song for guitar and changed numerous of the lyrics.

[15] Qtd. in Govenar, 53.

[16] Qtd. in Govenar, 53.

[17] Sam Hopkins, "Tim Moore's Farm," Gold Star 640/Modern 20-673, 1949.

[18] Sam Hopkins, "T Model Blues," Gold Star 662/Sittin' In With 644, 1949.

[19] Sam Charters, *The Country Blues* (New York: Da Capo Press, 1975), 266.

[20] See Govenar, 83.

[21] Qtd. in Governar, 236.

[22] Governar, 226ff.

[23] Sam Hopkins, "Got Nowhere to Lay My Head," in *My Life in the Blues,* Prestige Records, LP 7370, 1964.

# Chapter 9: Conclusion

Though emerging from the black American experience, the blues ultimately expresses elements of the universal human experience—mediated by particularities of the time and place of its origin. Thematically, blues artists sing of an array of topics, many that the more zealous of the black church-goers of the early 20th century found morally troubling. In general, the blues artists drew from their personal troubles to give their delivery of the blues an authenticity. Yet they were also performers, who expressed ideas that are not reducible to autobiography. As songwriters and performers, blues artists express ideas that they don't necessarily agree with. They assume diverse perspectives, display them and portray them. Many of the artists depicted contradictory views of the same topic. They played with themes, drawing at times from a stock of common linguistic and musical phrases, augmenting them as needed. Shakespeare does this, as do many other artists. We simply cannot identify a musical artist's views with the ideas communicated in an artist's lyrics, even if he or she has written those lyrics.

Artists interpret the world in stories. They share personal experiences as well as broader visions of the world with their audiences. Part of the appeal of the African American musicians of the period from which the music on the accompanying album comes is precisely that they give voice to common concerns, communicated stories relatable to their largely original

African American community. Many in these communities felt represented insofar as their similar stories, troubles and concerns were articulated. Bessie Smith epitomized this performative aspect of the blues—giving voice not only to her concerns but to the concerns of her community, especially women. Her stardom rose precisely because of the artistry that she honed in the black minstrel shows and that entranced an audience while entertaining it. But the performative was also basic for the country bluesmen highlighted here. Robert Johnson was an incredible performer, as was Lightnin' Hopkins. They, Skip James and the other artists discussed in this book and whose music is on the accompanying album all sang from experience. But that experience allowed them to create artwork—songs that expressed their perspectives and their experiences the ways artists express those things—and in ways that resonated with what Amiri Baraka has called "the blues people."

The blues artists were often in a position where it was tenuous to express explicit political criticism. Black artists had long learned to use veiled language. But in expressing stories about the economic and personal woes of their own lives and the lives of those around them, these artists helped create community. They created a sense of pride among their community and a sense of being represented because they were sharing the stories of that community.

Besides that, there is a kind of politics to the rejection of the major elements of the dominant moral system, false as it often is, and in the artist finding his or her own voice, expressive of the broader experience of a people. The blues documents broadly shared experiences of African American communities of the early 20th century. Yet it also is a musical form that has universal reach, resonating with emotion that is also part of the common stock of human experience. There is something specific about many of the stories of the blues. But there is something universal as well.

The blues also provided—and provides—a unique way for artists to work through their emotional travails. As we have seen, many of the early blues musicians found something spiritually fulfilling in this music, which allowed both the artists and their audience to turn their pain and anguish into beauty. They found in blues a kind of healing balm.

Few of the intellectuals of the early 20th century, white or black, were able to see the greatness of spirit of the simple country musicians, often with ill-formed manners and unhealed pains that affected their expression and moral sensibilities and the rhythms of their lives and music. In the end, many things changed this: the blues revival, the discovery of the diverse blues artists by rock'n'roll bands, the incorporation of blues into the various related forms—from boogie blues to jive blues to rhythm and blues. The often raw and simple blues music that developed in the early 20th century from African Americans cross-fed with other sources and changed our world, musically and otherwise. It did what John Hammond and a few insightful intellectuals like Langston Hughes were better able to see than most. It demonstrated the genius of a rural folk and created a universal art form out of a particular experience. It didn't bury its pain behind church hymns, false piety, and inherited dogmas, but aired its beautiful and often times afflicted reality, mirroring in part the broken, afflicted world. Yet it also transformed that brokenness in songs that allowed for the personal development of the artists who created them, while also giving a sense of community to an oppressed minority that had never before heard their own voices as a part of mainstream American life.

# References

Adorno, Theodor. *Minima Moralia: Reflections from Damaged Life.* Translated by E. F. N Jephcott. New York: Verso, 2005.

Albertson, Chris. *Bessie.* New Haven: Yale UP, 2003.

Baraka, Amiri. *Blues People: Negro Music in White America.* New York: Harper, 1999.

Blanks, Les, director. *The Blues According to Lightnin' Hopkins.* Les Blanks Films, 1970.

Calt, Stephen. *I'd Rather Be the Devil: Skip James and the Blues.* Chicago: Chicago Review Press, 2008.

Charters, Sam. *The Country Blues.* New York: Da Capo Press, 1975.

Conforth, Bruce M., and Gayle Dean Wardlow. *Up Jumped the Devil: The Real Life of Robert Johnson.* Chicago: Chicago Review Press, 2019.

Davis, Angela. *Blues Legacies and Black Feminism: Gertrude "Ma" Rainey, Bessie Smith and Billie Holiday.* New York: Vintage Books, 1998.

Du Bois, W.E.B. "Criteria of Negro Art." *The Crisis*, vol. 32, no. 6, 1926, pp. 290-297.

Evans, David. *Tommy Johnson.* Studio Vista, 1971.

---. *Big Road Blues.* New York: Da Capo Press, 1982.

Guralnick, Peter. *Looking to Get Lost. Adventures in Music & Writing.* New York: Little Brown and Company, 2020.

Garon, Paul. *Blues and the Poetic Spirit.* San Francisco: City Lights Books, 1996.

Gioia, Ted. *Delta Blues: The Life and Times of the Mississippi Masters Who Revolutionized American Music.* New York: Norton, 2008.

Gordon, Robert. *Can't Be Satisfied. The Life and Times of Muddy Waters.* New York: Little Brown and Company, 2002.

Govenar, Alan. *Lightnin' Hopkins: His Life and Blues.* Chicago: Chicago Review Press, 2010.

Handy, W. C. *Father of the Blues: An Autobiography*. New York: Da Capo Press, 1969.

Haymes, Max. "Catfish Blues (Origins of a Blues)," https://earlyblues. com/essay_catfish.htm. Accessed July 16, 2023.

Herzhaft, Gerard (1992). "Catfish Blues." *Encyclopedia of the Blues*. Fayetteville, Arkansas: University of Arkansas Press. https:// archive.org/details/encyclopediaofbl00herzh/page/442. Accessed June 21, 2024.

Hyatt, Harry M. *Hoodoo – Conjuration – Witchcraft – Rootwork*, vol. 1. Western Publishing, 1970.

James, Nehemiah "Skip". *Blues & the Soul of Man*. Stefan Grossman's Guitar Workshop, Inc., 2019.

Keaveny, Richard. "Aesthetics and the Issue of Identity." *The Critical Pragmatism of Alain Locke*, edited by Leonard Harris, Latham, Maryland: Roman & Littlefield, 1999.

Levering Lewis, David. *W.E.B. Du Bois: A Biography*. New York: Henry Holt, 2009.

Levine, Lawrence W. *Black Culture and Black Consciousness: Afro-American Folk Thought From Slavery to Freedom*. Oxford: Oxford UP, 2007.

Lord, Albert B. *The Singer of Tales*. 3rd ed., Cambridge, Mass: Harvard UP, 2020.

Mahan, Maureen. "How Bessie Smith Influenced a Century of Blues Music." *National Public Radio*, https://www.npr. org/2019/08/05/747738120/how-bessie-smith-influenced-a-century-of-popular-music. Accessed 17 July 2023.

McCormick, Robert "Mack." *Biography of a Phantom. A Robert Johnson Blues Odyssey*. Washington, DC: Smithsonian Books, 2023.

Nietzsche, Friedrich. *The Birth of Tragedy*, edited by Michael Tanner, translated by Shaun Whiteside. London: Penguin Books, 1993.

Oakley, Giles. *The Devil's Music. A History of the Blues*, 2nd ed. London: Da Capo Press, 1983.

The Obscure Origins of a Blues Classic, Catfish," www.knkx.org/jazz-and-blues/2013-07-19/obscure-origins-of-a-blues-classic-catfish-blues. Accessed April 24, 2024.

Ong, Walter. *Orality and Literacy.* 3rd ed., London: Routledge, 2012.

Oliver, Paul. *The Story of the Blues.* Boston: Northeastern UP, 1997.

Palmer, Robert. *Deep Blues.* New York: Viking Press, 1981.

Parry, Adam, editor. *The Making of Homeric Verse.* Oxford: Oxford UP, 1971.

Prial, Dunstan. *The Producer: John Hammond and the Soul of American Music.* New York: Farrar, Straus and Giroux, 2006.

Raboteau, Albert. *Slave Religion.* Oxford: Oxford UP, 2004.

Ratcliffe, Philip. *Mississippi John Hurt: His Life, His Times, His Blues.* Jackson: University of Mississippi Press, 2012.

Rogavia, Andria. "The Greatness of Lightning Hopkins" [online video compilation].

Slade, Paul. *Black Swan Blues: The Hard Rise and Brutal Fall of America's First Black-owned Record Label.* Planetslade.com, 2021.

Stewart, Jeffrey C. *The New Negro: The Life of Alain Locke.* Oxford: Oxford UP, 2018.

Tracy, Steven C. *Langston Hughes and the Blues.* Chicago: University of Illinois Press, 2001.

## Songs:

Hunter, Alberta, and Love Austin. "Downhearted Blues." Paramount, 1922.

Hurt, John Smith. "Pay Day." Vanguard, 1966

Hopkins, Sam. "Got Nowhere to Lay My Head." In *My Life in the Blues,* Prestige Records, LP 7370, 1964.

---. "Jail House Blues." Gold Star 662/Sittin' In With 644, 1949.

---. *My Life in the Blues,* Prestige Records. LP 7370, 1964.

---. "Shinin' Moon." Gold Star 613/Modern 20-543, 1947.

---. "That Mean Old Twister." Aladdin 167, 1946.

---. "Tim Moore's Farm." Gold Star 640/Modern 20-673, 1949.

---. "T Model Blues." Gold Star 662/Sittin' In With 644, 1949.

Jackson, Jim. "Jim Jackson's Kansas City Blues, Part 3." Vocalion, 1928.

James, Nehemiah "Skip." "22-20 Blues." Paramount Records, 1931.

---. "Devil Got My Woman." Paramount, 1931.

---. "Hard Time Killing Floor Blues." Paramount, 1931.

Johnson, Robert. "32-20 Blues." Vocalion, 1936.

---. "Come On In My Kitchen." Vocalion, July, 1937.

---. "Hellhound on My Trail." Vocalion, 1937.

---. "Love in Vain." Vocalion, 1936.

---. "Me and the Devil Blues." Vocalion, 1938.

---. "Phonograph Blues." Vocalion, 1936.

---. "When You Got a Good Friend." Vocalion, 1936.

---. "Walkin' Blues." Vocalion, 1936.

Johnson, Tommy. "Big Road Blues." Victor Records, 1928, V21279.

---. "Maggie Campbell Blues." Victor Records, 1928, V21409.

---. "Canned Heat Blues." Victor Records, 1928, V38535.

McLennan, Tommy. "Deep Blue Sea Blues." Bluebird Records, 1941.

McKinley Morgenfield, "Rolling Stone." Chess Records, 1950.

Petway, Robert. "Catfish Blues." Bluebird Records, 1941.

Smith, Bessie. "Backwater Blues." Columbia 14159D, Feb. 17, 1927.

---. "I Used to Be Your Sweet Mama." Columbia 14292D, Feb. 9, 1928.

Williams, D., Small, and T. Brymn. "Need a Little Sugar in My Bowl."
    Issued with Columbia, 1931.

**Darrell Arnold**

# About the Author

Darrell Arnold is philosopher and musician. While doing a dissertation in philosophy in Germany in the late 1990s and early 2000s, he recorded four CDs and regularly toured with his bands in Europe. Highlights included two tours as an opening band for the Yardbirds as well as festival gigs with Eric Burden and the New Animals, Alvin Lee, and Canned Heat. His most recent recording, prior to the release accompanying this book, is *Changing World*, produced by Jack Shawde.

Darrell's academic work has a focus on social political theory. He has translations in philosophy from German with Cambridge University Press and Columbia University Press and edited volumes with a focus on social theory with Routledge and Palgrave MacMillan.

## About the project contributors

### Irena Gapkovska

Irena takes inspiration from the moments and impressions from life: As she notes: "As a Macedonian artist, the influence of the Byzantine is present in my work in many different ways. My images are usually rather surrealistic in style, and I focus on the human figure in a symbolic manner. By using the aesthetics of ancient Macedonian art to express the spirituality of the subject, I make a bridge between abstract and figurative realities ~ combining them in an authentic manner with an intellectual approach to make a unique visual story."

Prior to Founding NGO Art Studio in Skopje, Macedonia in 1998, Irena was graphic designer for the newspaper Elena and for Nova Makedonija Magazine, receiving a national award for best art illustration. She earned a Master's Degree in Graphic Art from St. Kyril Methodiy University Fine Art Academy in Skopje. In addition to her studio in Skopje, she had a studio in Miami for ten years until 2018, when she relocated to Perpignan, France. She plays a Hohner Blues Harp.

## Jack Shawde

Jack Shawde is a Nashville-based guitarist, multi-instrumentalist and producer. Throughout his career, Jack has performed, recorded or toured with such legends as Bob Dylan, Dr. John, Paul Butterfield, Richie Havens, Stan Lynch (Tom Petty), Al Cooper (Blood Sweat & Tears), Bo Diddley, John Mayall, Chuck Berry and many more. Jack has performed and recorded all over the world, including accompanying Julio Iglesias at the Latin Grammy Awards, which were televised live to a worldwide audience of 10 million. He produced and played on Darrell's album, *Changing World,* as well as *Portraits of the Blues.*

## Don Sarley

*Portraits of the Blues* would not have been written with Don Sarley's inspiration. When Darrell approached Don about the possibility of working together with him to release his blues album, Don suggested publishing the album together with a book. Don is a partner of Y&T records, along with Rich Ulloa and Jim Wurster, and has established Arco Records as a blues label offshoot. He has been instrumental in helping get this book and album to market.

## Rose Gargiulo of Imagine Media Concepts

Imagine Media Concepts (IMC) is a design studio catering to artists, writers, and professionals throughout the United States and abroad. IMC is owned and operated by Rose Gargiulo, a South Florida multimedia designer who is also a guitarist and music producer. Rose regularly plays music with Darrell in Miami. She also formatted the book and did the cover layout for the book and album.

www.ingramcontent.com/pod-product-compliance
Lightning Source LLC
Chambersburg PA
CBHW060540130626
46553CB00002B/833